CHRONIC ILLNESS AND THE QUALITY OF LIFE

ANSELM L. STRAUSS, Ph.D.

Professor of Sociology,
University of California, San Francisco,
San Francisco, California

BARNEY G. GLASER, Ph.D.

Professor of Sociology,
University of California, San Francisco,
San Francisco, California

Saint Louis

THE C. V. MOSBY COMPANY

1975

Library of Congress Cataloging in Publication Data

Strauss, Anselm L
   Chronic illness and the quality of life.

   Bibliography: p.
   Includes index.
   1. Chronic diseases—Social aspects. 2. Chronic
diseases—Psychological aspects. 3. Chronically ill—
Care and treatment. I. Title. [DNLM: 1. Chronic
disease. WT500 S912c]
RA642.2.S76   362.1′04′22   75-2458
ISBN 0-8016-4837-8

GW/VH/VH   9   8   7   6   5

Chronic illness, or long-term illness as it is sometimes called, is here to stay. It will not vanish, despite the amazing advances in medical knowledge and technology. In fact, no matter how useful, helpful, or desirable, each advance (organ transplantation, for example) tends to bring in its wake certain new problems. Or it may simply, for specific persons, put off until another day the appearance of some relatively inevitable chronic condition. Not all conditions are fatal or even terribly discomforting; but many are and, as we shall shortly see, many "hit" fairly early in life and affect sizable portions of our population.

Many readers of this book—most of them health personnel, skilled at giving some specialized kind of care to the ill—will themselves be sufferers of one or more chronic conditions. These may plague them daily or occasionally prevent their working, until the condition eases up or is treated. If lucky enough not to have a chronic illness, then they are very likely to have a parent, spouse, child, or close friend who suffers from chronic illness. Indeed, that is most probable, given the great number of chronically ill people.

Stop a minute, then, and ask: How much do health personnel take into account their knowledge of chronic illness when caring for the ill persons who come to health facilities? How well do they translate their own experiential knowledge into their actual working with ill persons? Presumably the answer is that sometimes they act wisely on that experiential knowledge. Often, however, they do not. One reason for their failure is that the health facilities, as we shall discuss in Part Three, often, and perhaps even usually, do not especially reward them for employing that special wisdom. Beyond that, we ought to ask ourselves (the authors included) how much we really know about the problems of living to which certain chronic illness give rise. Our personal knowledge tends to be somewhat restricted, and that derived from our work tends to pertain to the experiences of ill persons while at the hospital, the clinic, or other health facility, rather than being rich in details about what life is like "back home," given their particular disease symptoms and their regimens.

This book has been written to acquaint readers with some of the enormous range of experiences associated with chronic illness. The book's focus is on the ill person, *and* his family, at *home*. The focus is also on how he and they manage to live as normal a life as possible in the face of his disease. So the emphasis is very much on the social and psychological aspects (not the medical) of *living with chronic illness*. In the terminology of an increasingly popular phrase: How is the *quality of life* affected by having a chronic disease?

Part One is devoted to a discussion of some of the major and complicated problems of living with chronic illness, including the management of crises, the handling of regimens, the controlling of symptoms, the handling of time and social isolation, and the attempt to live normally and maintain normal social relations.

Part Two consists of several studies of chronic conditions, drawn from the writings of our colleagues and students who are research nurses and sociologists, using data gathered from studies done under our direction or in consultation with us. These studies are intended to supplement the many quotations that appear in Part One, as well as the discussion in which they are embedded. They are intended, too, to dramatize the problems of managing regimens or controlling symptoms and the like and to further the empathy of readers.

Then, in Part Three, Chapter 15 is devoted to the question of how health personnel might obtain the kinds of biographical information needed from chronically ill patients in order to give better care. Chapter 16 touches on some of the larger issues of public policy with regard to the chronically ill.

As Professors of Sociology and for many years faculty members at the School of Nursing, University of California, San Francisco, we have been fortunate in being allowed free access to many health facilities and have been able to observe and interview a great many staff members. During one research project on terminal care in hospitals, we finally realized that most of the patients, terminal or not, were chronically ill—from cardiac diseases, cancer, asthma, and the like. As a result, eventually our students and we began to interview patients at their homes in order to see what life looked like from their viewpoint. This book and several research papers are the result of those studies. Understandably, we owe a very great deal to our students, research associates, and colleagues. We have drawn heavily on the interviews and field observations, particularly those of Jeanne Quint Benoliel, Marcella Z. Davis, Shizuko Fagerhaugh, Laura Reif, Barbara Suczek, and Carolyn L. Wiener, and very occasionally from those by George Chu and Theresa Louie. At the end of each field note quotation used, the researcher's name is given, except where it is our own. In addition, Chapters 9 through 14 are drawn from papers written by Carolyn L. Wiener, Laura Reif, Jeanne Quint Benoliel, Barbara Suczek, and Shizuko Fagerhaugh.

We are indebted to all of them, as well as to Barney Glaser's seminar on sociological analysis of qualitative data, and to Kathy Calkins Charmaz and Elihu

Gerson for stimulating conversations over the years about the social and psychological aspects of living with chronic disease. We also learned a great deal from the student nurses with whom we worked; from Anselm Strauss's course entitled "Chronic Disease" (three or four quotations from papers are included here; our apologies for not properly recording their names in our working notes <u>except Patricia E. Palmer</u>); from our colleague at the School of Nursing, Jeanne Hallberg; and from our friend and former colleague, Mildred McIntyre, who knows so much about both cardiac disease and those who suffer from it. We are also grateful to another friend and a medical colleague on our campus, Dr. Donald Fink. We must thank Helen Nahm, formerly Dean of the School of Nursing (but, more importantly, a wise woman), for commenting on a draft manuscript of this book. Our thanks also to the Russell Sage Foundation for generous funding of some of our research. Perhaps, most of all, we need and wish to thank the patients, their kinsmen, and the health personnel who have taught all of us by freely, so amazingly freely, giving us the information we needed. And without Fran, neither this book nor, quite literally the first-named author . . .

Anselm L. Strauss
Barney G. Glaser

CONTENTS

CHRONIC ILLNESS
AND THE QUALITY OF LIFE

INTRODUCTION

> In essence chronic illness is THE challenge of this era to hospital and public
> health officials, and to the medical, nursing, and other professions concerned
> with sickness and disability. . . . [It is] America's No. 1 health problem. . . .[5]

Those words were spoken in 1956 by L. Mayo, chairman of the famous
Commission on Chronic Illness, in a keynote address to a conference on chronic
illness, just on the eve of the Commission's influential four-volume report. The
Commission's definition of chronic diseases is still serviceable:

> All impairments or deviations from normal which have one or more of the
> following characteristics: are permanent, leave residual disability, are caused by
> non-reversible pathological alteration, require special training of the patient for
> rehabilitation, may be expected to require a long period of supervision, observa-
> tion, or care.[5]

A survey carried out during July, 1965 to June, 1967 by the Public Health
Service substantiates the prevalence of long-term illness as *the* major health
problem.[2] During the 2-year period of the survey, approximately 50 percent of the
civilian population, excluding residents in institutions, "had one chronic condition or more." Of those 94.9 million Americans, about 22 million "experienced
some degree of activity limitation and 6.3 million . . . had some form of mobility
limitation as a result of chronic conditions."

The magnitude of the activity and mobility problems is further suggested by
the following and more precise figures. About 4 million persons, or 2 percent of
our total population, were unable to carry on major activities (work, housekeep-
ing, school or preschool activities, participation in recreational, civic, or church
activities). Another 12 million were limited in major activity. Concerning mobility, or the ability to move about freely, about 1.4 million Americans were confined
to their houses except in emergencies; 1.8 million needed the help of others or
some special aid (cane, crutches, wheelchair) to move about; while still another 3
million persons had some trouble in "getting around freely."[2] As for the number of
chronic conditions per person, the average was 2.2—that is, *multiple* chronic
illnesses are very frequent.

Just what kinds of conditions are chronic? The authors of the survey give these figures:

Heart conditions	16.4%
Arthritis and rheumatism	14.8
Impairments of back or spine	8.2
Mental and nervous conditions	7.8
Impairments of lower extremities and hips	6.1
Visual impairments	5.6
Hypertension without heart involvement	5.4

People of different ages are likely to suffer from different chronic conditions. For example, the two chief conditions affecting mobility limitation are:

Under 17 years:	Paralysis, complete or partial	28.2%
	Impairments of lower extremities and hips	15.3
17 to 44 years:	Paralysis, complete or partial	13.6
	Impairments of lower extremities and hips	13.6
45 to 64 years:	Arthritis and rheumatism	25.1
	Heart conditions	13.0
65 years and over:	Arthritis and rheumatism	29.3
	Heart conditions	15.4

Although as long ago as 1956 Mayo pointed to a common misconception about chronic illness—namely that it is synonymous with old age[1]—probably most laymen and health professionals too tend to share that misconception. It is true that elderly people are much more likely to have chronic conditions (and more of them), but it is not at all true that chronic disease is merely a geriatric problem. The survey's figures show the following:

Persons having no chronic conditions:

Under 17 years	77.2%
17 to 44 years	45.9
45 to 64 years	28.9
65 years and over	14.4

Persons with one chronic condition or more,
  some or total limitation in a major activity:

Under 17 years	0.9%
17 to 44 years	4.7
45 to 64 years	14.2
65 years and over	39.5

Thus even very young children can be afflicted, while youthful to middle-aged persons are in no small measure quite impaired.

The magnitude of many of those figures is certainly startling. The next question is: to what is due the size of the chronic disease problem? In part, it is due, as one social researcher notes, to the sheer increase of the American population: more people, more chronic disease.[1] In part it is attributable to a larger portion of elderly people in the population. Unquestionably, however, the major factor in the growing prevalence of long-term illness is the impressive elimination or control of infectious and parasitic diseases. At least in the industrialized nations of the world, including the Soviet Union, these no longer afflict or even kill large proportions of the population. Now we in those nations die from such illnesses as cancer and the various heart conditions and suffer in great numbers from such diseases as arthritis, diabetes, Parkinson's disease, multiple sclerosis, epilepsy, or other neurological diseases.

Given all that, it is rather strange that health personnel—from physicians "on down"—still tend to refer to the hospitals as places where acute illness is treated, while people with chronic illness are housed mainly at special facilities, such as nursing homes, and of course are treated as ambulatory at the physicians' offices, clinics, and community health centers.

It is perhaps the disease-oriented training and interests of the health professionals that lead them to refer to hospitalized patients as acutely ill. After all, the shoulder-to-shoulder battle against fatal or at least crippling disease is a deservedly recognizable part of modern medicine. Yet even cursory scrutiny shows that most patients visiting the hospital for specialized treatments are not there because of acute diseases but because they currently suffer from an acute phase of one or another chronic disease: cancer, cardiac, kidney, respiratory, and the like.

This is no particular news, for hospital staffs actually do realize that many, if not most, of their patients have diseases for which a genuine cure does not exist. What can only be accomplished is, in common parlance, mainly "checking the progress of the disease," "getting them back on their feet," "slowing up the inevitable," and so on. If pressed, most personnel would agree that they were not engaged in "cure" in the old-fashioned sense of curing pneumonia or measles.

Nevertheless, they tend to reserve the contrasting term "care" for those patients whom one can only make more comfortable, who definitely seem so "chronic," their condition so "hopeless," so bad that "nothing much can be done," that they belong somewhere other than in a highly specialized work place such as a hospital. That is why one researcher recently could report that hospitalized stroke patients seemed, from the staff's viewpoint, to be out of place.[3] Or, in the somewhat plaintive words of Dr. Steinberg, the Director of Mount Sinai Hospital in New York, some years ago:

> I am a director of a general hospital for the treatment of the acute, not chronic diseases. In such an atmosphere, chronic disease is an accusation . . . . On the one hand . . . there is a movement to begin to widen the hospital's usefulness [to chronic patients]. On the other hand, we are frustrated because of the difficulty of carrying out our primary mission—the treatment of acute disease.[5]

These contrasts of acute/chronic and cure/care reflect something of a paradox so characteristic of contemporary health care. On the one hand, health personnel can believe, and assert with conviction, that chronic disease is the number one problem. On the other hand, they can continue to think about conquering chronic disease (and handling the number one problem) in terms not much different than when the prevalent diseases were genuinely communicative or parasitic.

Of course, it is perfectly true that some chronic diseases eventually will be conquered and even prevented, but perhaps not all and certainly most of them not very soon.

However, the astonishing progress of medical technology allows us to hope for conquered disease and increased longevity. Understandably, those people who aid in progress toward that magnificent goal are given special rewards and honors. Those who merely help to care for, to give comfort to, the incurably ill tend to get far less money and prestige for their efforts, whatever may be the psychological rewards accruing to the work. Additionally, in countries where specialization is far advanced and where specialists usually have great prestige or even great glamour, the organization of medical care and health care tends to be along categorical lines (heart, cancer, stroke, and so on), rather than focused on chronic disease in general.

Why should the focus not be in categorical terms? After all, specialists in neurological disease, for example, will best understand and battle such disease, not specialists in skin disease or some other bodily part or system far removed from the brain functions! Furthermore, even in terms of public support (in the United States) for attacks on given diseases, money can best be raised and research effectively concentrated if the public interest is sharply focused. In the words of Mary Switzer, a former director of the Office of Vocational Rehabilitation, it is all very well to talk of rehabilitation in general, but to be practical one must:

> ... recognize that we would not be as far along the road as we are now if we did not have the emotional investment that has gone into the development of "special interest" programs .... It is ... important that special groups strike out and dramatize specific problems like polio, cancer and mental illness.[5]

Many people would argue persuasively that agencies organized across-the-board, rather than along somewhat limited disease lines (cardiac, respiratory), would simply be and are ineffective.

Against such considerations, it is possible to make two arguments. The first: to treat medically the problems of any chronically ill patient, one has to supplement the strictly medical knowledge with psychological and social knowledge—about the patient's family and other intimates, as well as about the patient himself. That knowledge will include not only how he and they handle his disease and the associated medical regimens but how his disease, regimens, and symptoms affect his and their lives—and so possibly, or even probably, the ultimate progress of his disease. Presumably, however, different chronic diseases will have different impacts on their victims' lives. Thus, although not strictly medical, this is still a categorical approach to all persons. However, the current categorical approach is mainly, often totally, medical; hence, it tends to hamper thinking about *chronic disease* in more than a piecemeal—one at a time or one group at a time—fashion. This point can be illustrated graphically by the following case report as summarized by a somewhat astonished pediatrician[4]:

Rickey is a three-and-one-half-year-old boy residing in Baltimore City. His mother was afflicted with German measles in the first trimester of her pregnancy. Rickey was born with the full-blown picture of the rubella syndrome. He had congenital cataracts and congenital heart disease. He developed a bleeding disorder (thrombocytopenic purpura) and hemolytic anemia. His blood disorders improved, and he began to gain weight. Heart surgery was done at age three-and-one-half months, and he was finally discharged.

Rickey showed slow motor and mental development. He was essentially blind, and it became apparent that he was also deaf. He developed an intolerance to milk and required a special soybean formula. At age twenty months, after close study, a hearing aid was prescribed and obtained. Soon after, his cataracts were removed surgically. He has been evaluated and followed by the director of admissions of the School for the Blind. He attends the Gateway Pre-school for communication disorders . . . .

The agencies, clinics, and services from which Rickey is receiving services are as follows:

Baltimore City Health Department
  Western Health District, Well Baby Clinic
  Division for the Handicapped
Maryland State Department of Health
  Division of Crippled Childrens' Services
  Division for Community Services to the Mentally Retarded
The Johns Hopkins Hospital
  Cardiac Clinic
  Hearing and Speech Center
  Child Growth and Development Study
  Wilmer Eye Clinic
  Pediatric Clinic
  Emergency Room
Greater Baltimore Medical Center
  Comprehensive Pediatric Clinic
The Childrens' Hospital
  Orthopedic Clinic
The Hearing and Speech Agency of Metropolitan Baltimore
  The Gateway Pre-school
The School for the Blind
  Mrs. Minturn, Director of Admissions
Day Care Services for the Mentally Retarded (tentative)
Rosewood State Hospital (tentative)

It has come to the attention of the staff of one of the involved agencies that the family of this child is being run to death and has incurred considerable expenses despite multiple resources for assistance. Virtually without a break, this mother had continuous appointments over a two-week period . . . .

This child has received regular follow-up for his various diagnostic problems. However, his family is run ragged and so near the end of its rope that they are considering institutional placement despite the inappropriateness of such placement. . . .

> ... Many of the services given this child just grew, like Topsy. Countless medical summaries and notes exist, but they are scattered in the records of several facilities.
>
> It is neither a popular nor a constructive attitude to criticize the weaknesses of a system without enumeration of its strengths and assets. Rickey's case illustrates the strengths in the abundance of willing hands, the adequacy of specialized skills, and the appropriate utilization of a number of resources designed to help the child in his special areas of need. However, somehow the family got lost sight of, and through this loss, all the efforts, time, expense, and personal commitment may go down the drain.

The second argument against a strictly categorical approach rests on the fact that persons who are chronically ill share many social and psychological problems. Of course, each disease or group of diseases also brings different social and psychological problems. Nevertheless, an understanding of the common, rather than only the different, problems can be of considerable aid in improving the lives of the chronically ill. These common problems are complex and need to be studied and their implications thought through for particular patients and groups of patients.

In advancing these two arguments, we do not mean to deny the usefulness of a strictly categorical approach. We are, however, asserting that a more general approach also can be very useful; it could help to shift some of the focus from rather strictly medical matters—and from the acute phases of chronicity—to the daily lives of the chronically ill and their families. Without understanding a great deal about how the chronically ill get through their days outside of health facilities, health personnel will never understand what they really need to know in order to give effective care at the facilities—and to ensure that the patients will not return more quickly than they should.

Of course it would be foolish, and downright incorrect, to believe that physicians, nurses, social workers, physical therapists, occupational therapists, and other health personnel know nothing about the personal lives of chronically ill patients and their families. Many a patient is an open book to those who attend him. But, of course, many a patient is a closed book, too! More to the point, however, is that the training of health personnel is rarely focused upon social and psychological matters (every reader will find exception to that statement, but generally speaking, it is true). Worse yet, at the health facilities, the staff's accountability is for medical and procedural actions, not particularly for those pertaining to psychological and social matters—witness the charting and the reporting.[6] A log of nonmedical information (most of it oral in nature) does build up on particular patients, but that information mainly tends to be couched in terms that competent psychologists or sociologists (or perhaps psychiatrists) would often find more harmful than genuinely useful for effective health care.

As for an informative literature bearing on the daily social and psychological problems of the chronically ill and their families, it is fairly sparse. The vast literature about various of the diseases pertains mainly to their medical aspects and to their medical management. Much discussion about the emotional and personal concomitants of chronic disease tends to be anecdotal and experiential rather than researched or deeply studied. The information is better than nothing, but all too often it does not add up to very much.

Of course some diseases—like asthma—seem to have psychological components and so have been studied by psychiatrists and psychologists. But to understand how a given disease affects the daily experiences of the afflicted persons, one is likely to find better information in the occasional autobiographies written by patients than in the standard literature about their diseases.

While the detailed medical discussions of etiology, symptomatology, treatment, and regimens often do touch on the social consequences for the patient and his family, generally there is not much focus upon how he and they might better manage their lives, given the particular disease. There is little focus, either, on how health workers might help with the problems that come in the wake of chronic illness and their treatments—problems like social stigmatization of the patient, isolation, family disruption, marital discord, transformation of domestic roles—or even the seemingly more medical matters like how to prevent fatal physiological crises through making necessary arrangements within the family or in the neighborhood.

Gradually more attention is being paid to the social and psychological aspects of chronic disease by psychiatrists (as in recent studies of the families of children dying of leukemia), by nurse scientists (as represented in Part Two of this book), and by behavioral scientists. Nevertheless, there is still a paucity of literature that can be drawn upon for obtaining either an intimate feeling for the problems of the chronically ill or systematic knowledge about their problems in general.

A FRAMEWORK

How can we begin to think about long-term illnesses in terms that are not strictly medical? How can we learn to see with some directness and clarity the *social* and *psychological* problems faced by the chronically ill (and their immediate families) in their daily lives?

To begin to get both an empathy with the ill and some effective ways of thinking systematically about their experiences, we suggest the following framework.

First of all, one must think of any given disease as potentially causing *multiple problems* of daily living for the person so unfortunate as to have the disease. Among those problems are:

1. The prevention of *medical crises* and their management once they occur
2. The control of *symptoms*
3. The carrying out of prescribed *regimens* and the management of problems attendant upon carrying out the regimens
4. The prevention of, or living with, *social isolation* caused by lessened contact with others

5. The adjustment to changes in the *course of the disease*, whether it moves downward or has remissions
6. The attempts at *normalizing* both interaction with others and style of life
7. *Funding*—finding the necessary money—to pay for treatments or to survive despite partial or complete loss of employment

These are among the *key problems*. It takes no great imagination to see why. For instance, if a dying cancer patient and his family cannot adjust to his downward course or to the swings of his good and bad days or weeks, then they are all in for psychological and domestic trouble. Or if a regimen necessitates radical changes in life style (as when a person with heart trouble is forbidden to smoke, drink, or eat sweets), that medical injunction is likely to have a considerable impact on his social and perhaps domestic life.

To handle such key problems, patients and their kinsmen and friends must develop *basic strategies*. They must work out standard methods or techniques that will yield some measure of success with those key problems. For instance, a person with cardiac disease may have to avoid even slight inclines and so must learn to route himself through his neighborhood streets, even if this means taking "the long way around." Or someone with ulcerative colitis may have to develop techniques of unexpectedly excusing himself from social occasions for several minutes without causing any suspicion of what he has to do after he gets to the bathroom.

Many of these strategies call for the assistance of family and friends, or even acquaintances and strangers. These act as various kinds of *agents*. Thus, in the pages to follow, we shall see people who act as *rescuing* agents (saving a diabetic individual from dying when he is in a coma), or as *protective* agents (accompanying an epileptic person so that if he begins to fall he can be eased to the ground), or as *assisting* agents (helping with a regimen), or as *control* agents (making the patient stay with his regimen), and so on.

The basic strategies for coping with the key problems call for certain kinds of *organizational* or *family arrangements*. People's efforts must be coordinated—with all the understandings and agreements which that necessitates. Thus disabled patients have standing arrangements with neighbors and friends who do their grocery shopping for them. The parents of diabetic children need to coach neighbors in reading the signs of oncoming coma as well as to warn them against allowing the child to have sweets while at their homes. A cardiac husband and his wife may reach an agreement—perhaps only after much persuasion by her—that when she senses his oncoming fatigue before he does, she will warn him; otherwise he may suddenly and embarrassingly run out of energy. Clearly, to establish and maintain such necessary arrangements may require not only much trust and considerable interactional skill but also financial, medical, and familial resources. If any of those are lacking, the arrangements may never get properly instituted or may collapse. In any case, important *consequences*—for both the patient and his family—flow from how he and they have organized their efforts so as to handle his key problems.

In sum, then, the important terms in our framework for understanding the daily experiences of chronically ill persons include key problems, basic strategies, family and organizational arrangements, and the consequences of those arrangements. We reluctantly add that health personnel are, in this scheme, far from the only important features. True, they can be crucial for some persons' very survival and also may give very useful counsel or aid in managing their key problems. However, realistically (as we shall see especially in Part Two), medicine as currently constituted tends to be distinctly secondary—if contributory—to the patient's day-to-day "carrying on" in the face of his disease. A major reason for this book, however, is the increasing interest of health personnel in the difficulties facing the chronically ill and their desire to be of assistance in the handling of those difficulties.

Let us turn now to separate discussions of the key problems listed. Those problems are not strikingly different from the ones confronted by normal people when occasionally they fall acutely ill; but readers should soon see, if they cannot yet imagine, why the problems of chronicity are perhaps qualitatively different. This is so if only because of the wearing persistence and relative permanence of these problems. While normal persons, once they are over their acute illness, can soon forget it, the chronically sick cannot forget; their illnesses are either always with them or, if quiescent, potentially lurking just around the corner.

In this book, we shall be at pains to emphasize that it is not only the sick person who faces these problems but also, in all likelihood, his immediate family. His fate is, in a real sense, also theirs. We shall signalize their mutual struggle—to manage their living despite his chronicity—by referring most often to him as a sick person rather than primarily as "the patient."

REFERENCES

1. Bright, Margaret: Demographic background for programing for chronic diseases in the U.S. In Lilienfeld, A., and Gifford, A., editors: Chronic disease and public health, Baltimore, 1966, Johns Hopkins Press, pp. 5-22.
2. Chronic conditions and limitations of activity and mobility, U.S., July 1965-June 1967, Public Health Service Publication No. 1000, Series 10-61, U.S. Department of Health, Education, and Welfare, Public Health Services, Mental Health Administration, January, 1971, pp. 1-4, 8, 11.
3. Hoffman, Joan: Nothing can be done, Urban Life and Culture 3:50-70, 1974.
4. Hopkins, Edward: The chronically ill child and the community. In Debuskey, M., editor: The chronically ill child and his family, Springfield, Illinois, 1970, Charles C Thomas, Publisher, pp. 196-198.
5. Mayo, L.: Problem and challenge. In Guides to action on chronic illness, New York, 1956, National Health Council, pp. 9-13, 35, 55.
6. Strauss, Anselm, Glaser, Barney, and Quint, Jeanne: The non-accountability of terminal care, Hospitals 38:73-87, 1964.

PROBLEMS OF LIVING WITH CHRONIC ILLNESS

CHAPTER 1

PREVENTING AND MANAGING MEDICAL CRISES

Crisis. This is a striking place to begin our discussion, since it seems quite medical; yet so much that is social is involved in how crises are prevented and managed, and even in how they get triggered.

Some chronic diseases are, of course, especially characterized by potentially fatal medical crises. Cardiac conditions are rather obvious instances of that point, as is severe diabetes, which may lead to insulin comas from which the diabetic individual may not emerge alive unless rescued in time. In contrast, epileptic convulsions may not kill the person unless his breath gets totally cut off, but the convulsions may occur so suddenly that he is endangered by his falling or by moving automobiles. In order to actually prevent these crises—when that is possible—and to minimize their potentially fatal effects when they do occur, the vulnerable person, and probably his close kinsmen too, must organize his and their lives for crisis management. They must literally construct and maintain necessary organizational arrangements. After a given crisis, they may need to reconstitute or to improve those arrangements.

Relevant to crises are these questions. How probable is their recurrence? How far can they go (to or short of death)? How frequent are they? How fast do they appear? How clear are the signs of their coming to the patient or kinsmen or bystanders or even health personnel? Can they be prevented or their effects mitigated and by whom? How expected are their appearances? How complex are the rescue operations? What resources are available to prevent the crisis or to pull the person through it relatively undamaged or at least alive? The following discussion will touch on these questions.

READING THE SIGNS

First, let us look at the organization of effort that can be involved in properly reading signs that portend crisis. Thus diabetic people or the parents of diabetic children are taught by health personnel not only how to prevent potential crises (caused either by sugar shortage or by insulin shock) but how to recognize the signs of oncoming crisis itself. They are also taught what to do in case of an actual crisis. In turn, diabetic individuals or their parents teach their kinsmen, friends, and possibly their neighbors, school teachers, and fellow workers what to see and do when the crisis is appearing or actually occurs. Likewise, epileptic persons and sufferers from sickle cell disease, if they are so fortunate as to have signs immediately preceding their convulsions, learn to recognize the signs and so prepare themselves for the oncoming crisis. They sit down, lie down, and if in public get themselves to a place of safety.

To prevent mistakes on the part of others when in crisis, or to get proper action that will save themselves, diabetic individuals may carry instructions on their persons. If they do not, bystanders won't read the signs correctly and so won't know what to do or may do the wrong thing. As a book on ileostomy warns:

> Fluid or electrolyte imbalance is the most serious danger to the ileostomy patient. It can occur very precipitously and endanger the patient's life within a day. Its cause is excessive output through the ileostomy. . . . A simple case of flu, partial obstruction, or an accident may initiate increased . . . output. For this reason diarrhea lasting more than twelve hours must be reported to a physician. It is recommended that every ileostomy patient carry an ID card giving in addition to personal identification the name of the condition, describing briefly the method of appliance removal and skin care, and listing the name and number of surgeon or hospital to contact for information in case of an accident. Ileostomy is still a rare condition and may not even be recognized by hospital personnel.[2]

Ironically enough, if the disease is rare or relatively unknown to them, physicians may even sometimes read noncrisis signs incorrectly and so precipitate a fatal medical crisis. This can happen, for instance, when a person with sickle cell disease is brought bleeding and unconscious to a hospital and immediate effort is made to stop the bleeding—because he has failed to carry instructions *not* to stop the bleeding!

Like properly instructed ileostomy patients, diabetic persons may carry not only instructions but also materials with which they or others can counteract their crisis: sugar or candy or insulin. A man with epilepsy may stuff a handkerchief between his teeth just before convulsions, and a knowledgeable bystander may know enough to open his jaws, get his tongue out if necessary, and employ a handkerchief.

When signs are not read properly, are read too slowly, or are interpreted as meaning something else, then people die or come close to dying. This is what happens when comas are mistaken for fainting or alcoholic convulsions. This also is what happens when a person with cardiac disease for the first time experiences severe chest pains but passes them off as unimportant or as merely signs of a bad cold. (Thereafter, he may put his doctor's name and telephone number right under the telephone—and carry the information in his wallet, too—for emergency use.) When an unconscious patient is brought into the emergency room of the nearest hospital, physicians there understandably may treat him for the wrong disease. Indeed, any crisis-prone person brought to an emergency room runs the hazard of being misdiagnosed unless he is either conscious—and so can talk to the physicians—or carries something on his person that will alert them to his disease. Otherwise, the staff is at a great disadvantage because an adequate medical history is lacking.

A slower version of the same diagnostic error is when patients with cancer are misdiagnosed; only later may the correct diagnosis be made, often too late to save the patient. Moreover, not only may a patient misread his own signs but also the associated signs of crucially assisting machinery; thus inexperienced patients who are on kidney dialysis machinery may not recognize that their machinery is not working correctly and may not realize that their bodies therefore are nearing physiological crisis. Errors also can be committed even by quite experienced persons, because they have not yet learned to recognize that biological changes in their bodies—for instance, changes caused by the life cycle—can bring about crisis, so they read the signs as noncritical.

ORGANIZING FOR CRISES

That nonmedical organization of effort is necessary for preventing or managing crises should be apparent from what we have touched on before, but the point is worth further amplification. Not only must danger signs be read correctly and appropriate actions be taken by the person himself or by other people; additional kinds of organized actions—some relatively simple, some very complex—may be necessary. Thus, it is imperative that a crisis-prone diabetic man or woman *not* leave the house without candy or insulin, otherwise he or she may be unable to prevent or overcome the crisis. On weekends, care must be taken that there is insulin in the house, because then most pharmacies are closed. The mother of a diabetic child needs to make special arrangements for insulin shots and proper diet with the mother of his chums if he is to stay overnight at their house.

> One mother has arranged to have her epileptic adult daughter live with her own friends, because someone must, the mother believes, live with her constantly. Once the daughter went out alone and had to be rescued from the traffic. The friends with whom she lives now do not allow her, during heavy traffic hours, to cross a boulevard in the neighborhood for fear of her either being hit or having an epileptic fit then and there.   *Palmer*

Mr. James, who had a cardiac condition:

> described how the phone numbers of an ambulance, his doctor, and his wife at work could be taped to the phone. He would plan to contact them in that order if he felt an attack coming on. He reemphasized that he could tell when one was approaching. Also he would not lock the front door so that if he would be unable to let the ambulance people in, they could get to him.

The adherence to crisis-preventing regimens may require, as with cystic fibrosis or kidney dialysis patients, a high degree of daily organization in the family. With such a disease as hemophilia, the entire environment may have to be controlled minutely so that the child does not stumble against sharp edges and begin his fatal bleeding; so too must the adults institute over the child an ever-vigilant guard.

> The young hemophiliac son of Czar Nicholas of Russia had two servants to hover constantly over him and catch him if he began to fall. Sometimes he wore padded suits, and even the trees in the area where he played were padded in the event that he might brush against them.[3]

In fact, the parents of a hemophiliac child wage continual war against both a potentially fatal environment and against the potentially fatal actions of the child himself. This kind of intense monitoring of the child's bodily activity and the environs can lead not only to his excessive dependency but to great friction between a resentful child and the parents as protective agents. The parents cannot even resort to mild corporal punishment if the child is disobedient.

It is worth adding that in all the examples just noted, the potential danger of death is great, as is the relative speed with which the crisis can both occur and go through to death. This eventuality can, however, be prepared against, although not always successfully, because it is relatively expectable. Certainly the specific time of a crisis may take everyone by surprise. Nevertheless, since the event is expectable, organizing against its occurrence can be fairly effective.

BREAKDOWN OF ORGANIZATION: POTENTIAL AND ACTUAL

When the crisis is not so foreseeable, then it is more likely to prove disastrous, since usually there is less organization of effort to manage it. A crisis may be unexpected not only because of the nature of the specific disease but because of the inexperience or medical ignorance of the sick person and his family.

> One cardiac man interpreted his physician's instructions to stop working as meaning just that, but he did not discontinue his daily exercise, which consisted of heavy weight lifting and bicycle riding. He could have precipitated a fatal crisis, although he did not. Doubtless his physician would have been very upset—or at least exasperated—if he had known how his instructions were interpreted!

If the onset of a disease has begun with a visible medical crisis, bringing fear but awareness to the patient, then of course he and his family are more likely to make careful arrangements against the possibility of crisis recurrence. The more likely are they, also, to get the willing cooperation of friends and extended kinsmen, who can easily believe in the legitimacy of his requests concerning their help to prevent another crisis. If there had been no such original crisis, however, the attending health personnel may have to impress on him and his family that such a danger really does exist.

> A cardiac patient of our acquaintance surprises his friends by answering "no" honestly when they ask him if he had been afraid of death during his myocardial infarction; concomitantly, though he takes the precaution of carrying his

cardiologist's telephone number in his wallet, he really does not, "in his guts," believe himself likely to have any emergency.

Understandably, too, the further away patients are from the experience of an actual crisis, the more likely they are to relax their guard. They are "out of the woods." This can be seen right in the hospital a few days after a patient's myocardial infarction. After the patient is feeling better, he begins to move around more than the staff believes he should. They reprimand him; that is, essentially they tell him to organize his behavior more in accordance with his crisis-prone condition. On the other hand, one can also see the staff begin, in their turn, to relax their vigilance as they pay increasingly less attention to him in favor of more critically ill competitors. Interestingly enough, sometimes the patient believes he is out of danger sooner than does the staff and sometimes vice versa, so that some patients are warned repeatedly to take it easy (and sometimes threatened with the imagery of death if they do not), while other patients who seem overly frightened of dying are urged to move around more, not to be afraid, and generally to stop acting so unrealistically sick. When the patient gets home, the same dramas may, and probably will, be reenacted with his family.

Assuming there is an organization of effort for crisis management, any breakdown or disruption of it can be disastrous. Thus family strain can lead to the abandonment of or lessening of control over crisis-preventing regimens. The temporary absence of protective agents or of control agents (mothers, in the instance of diabetic children who are prone to eat too much candy) can be disastrous. A divorce or separation that leaves an assisting agent (a mother assisting her child with cystic fibrosis with absolutely necessary exercises) alone, unrelieved with her task, can gradually or quickly lead to a crisis. (One divorced couple, however, arranged matters so that the husband would relieve his wife on weekends and on some evenings.) Even an agent's illness can lead to the relaxation of regimens or the elimination of actions that might otherwise prevent crisis. Other things being equal, though, slow onsets of crises do allow for the remobilization of disrupted organization. Clear signs of crisis are likely to allow more effective remobilization than do unclear signs.

The worst situation, however, is when a sick person is abandoned by kinsmen and friends, so that the only effort he can call on against potential crises is his own. If he cannot even count on himself, then he or his family may purchase the efforts of necessary agents, but if money runs out then the following kind of situation (reported on in the *San Francisco Chronicle*, April 10, 1971) can occur:

> A man dying from a rare form of epilepsy and who needs constant attendant care to stay alive received help from the State yesterday.
> Medi-Cal chief Dr. Earl Brian authorized the immediate hospitalization of John Herbert Roberts, 42, who is in a convalescent home, for "current evaluation" of his needs.
> Roberts, who is suffering from myoclonic epilepsy, needs constant attendant care to assure that he doesn't choke to death during spasms.

> Dr. Julian Milestone, Roberts' doctor, said, "he could die any time, if there is no one in the room to watch him, he could die in five minutes."
>
> Medi-Cal pays $400 a month for Roberts' stay in the home but would not pay the $1000 a month needed for an attendant 15 hours a day.
>
> Roberts' relatives and friends had paid for the attendant care in the past but they said their money ran out yesterday.[4]

Six months later, however, Mr. Roberts won a state Supreme Court case against Medi-Cal, the judge ruling mercifully that:

> Since petitioner suffers from a unique illness, with abnormal requirements (for treatment), his claim does not quite fit within any of the pigeon holes (created by Medi-Cal regulations). Respondent could, of course, issue new regulations taking account of petitioner's plight, but he has not done so.
>
> Respondent's argument stops here . . . but the inevitable, if unspoken, conclusion is that petitioner will not receive the nursing care he needs and regretably, will die. . . .
>
> Fortunately . . . neither the statutes nor regulations compel so horrific a result.[5]

In some disease conditions, the ill person believes he cannot count on others, no matter how alert and well disposed, to prevent his dying—because realistically they cannot. "Once again I found it difficult to fall asleep," writes a cardiac patient recovering from his first heart attack. "I would lie awake thinking for hours. Would I get over it? What more was in store for me? I had nightmares. . . ."[1] Well he might, thinking he might never wake up! Again, when people suffer from myasthenia gravis, when skeletal muscles become flaccid, there is the possibility of their choking through loss of tongue control.

> One patient who takes a drug that temporarily corrects his drastic muscular defect—and which wears off rapidly after a few hours—must wake twice during sleeping hours in order to take it. When occasionally he has overslept, he has barely been able to swallow or even breath. Understandably he is in great fright over the possibility of choking to death.

An especially poignant instance of virtually constant guarding against medical crisis is the plight of people who suffer from very extreme emphysema. The slightest psychological upset can rob them of their vital but scarce oxygen, so they tend completely to avoid social contact and interaction with other people. Any kind of emotion, even laughing, might bring them into crisis. In short, when the patient is his own protective agent, he carries a very heavy burden.

The self-against-fate feeling, and experience, can be contrasted with the experience of individuals who can really do relatively little about potential crises (other than to follow their regimens faithfully), but who must rely almost solely on their physicians' skilled efforts to prevent or manage crises. Kidney transplant patients are a good example. Some are immensely trustful of and grateful to their surgeons; it is easy to see why.

POSTCRISIS PERIOD

Now, just a word about the postcrisis period in relation to the organization of efforts. At home, of course, such patients require plenty of family organization to prevent additional crises or to manage them if they occur. What is not so evident is that signs of improvement may be read, by kinsman or patient, when few exist; or that a hundred and one contingencies may arise that render faulty the organization for further crisis prevention and crisis management. Relevant variables here are how far back and rapid are the recovery, since both of these may vary for different disease conditions. Paradoxically, some crises-to-death allow for rather speedy recovery (insulin shock), while others that may be far less dangerous, or at least have proceeded less far, allow the person to feel and act "normal" only after some days or weeks have elapsed. Postcrisis organization is correspondingly affected, being relaxed more quickly or maintained alertly for much longer.

If, indeed, there is yet another crisis and one or more parties to crisis arrangements believe the arrangement was faulty, then there can be considerable guilt or anger, depending upon who feels at fault and who feels angrily virtuous. Control agents who failed or who were disobeyed, protective agents who were not sufficiently alert to the signs of crisis or who were outwitted by careless patients, these are the kinds of actors in the crisis drama who are likely to feel guilty or aggrieved and angry. Unfortunately, these reactions can have a negative impact on domestic relations and hence on the family's ability to manage future crises.

CEDING RESPONSIBILITY TO THE HOSPITAL

It is worth adding that when a sick person is brought to the hospital just prior to or during a period of crisis, he and his family are, in effect, ceding responsibility for crisis management to the hospital's personnel. The family's crisis organization gives way to professional organization. Those patients who have been fighting against potential crises (such as cancer victims nearing the ends of their lives) may cede control with a sense of relief. Carrying the burden was just too much. However, sometimes such delegation to hospital personnel can be difficult for patients and even devastating to their sense of personal worth, since they no longer appear to themselves to be competent in handling their own affairs. On a less tragic scale, this same phenomenon can be observed with patients with ulcerative colitis when they enter the hospital. They are accustomed to close monitoring of their symptoms and to the prevention of potential crises by careful adherence to regimens, and they only enter the hospital when their condition becomes critical. Then their monitoring functions are quickly taken over by the hospital staff. Typically, the staff is quite unaware that the almost total delegation of control to itself can be damaging to the patient's identity. The delegation may be necessary, but it is usually not cushioned by softening gestures.

Furthermore, when the staff thinks the repeated hospitalization of specific patients is caused by personal or familial negligence, then it tends to look with some disfavor on those patients. An extreme example, of course, is the distaste that the personnel of emergency rooms have for alcoholic "repeaters," even when brought to the site in bad condition. Much more subtle is the staff's response when faced by such a situation as the following:

> Two hemophiliac men, respectively 26 and 27 years old, are called "crocks" by the staff, because they pretty frequently come back in crisis state and have to be given one more transfusion. Nobody really knows much about them, except that they seem "queer."

Well might they seem queer, having gone through a lifetime of potentially fatal crises! More to the point, however, is that the staff feels frustrated, since it feels not as if these patients were saved through skilled or efficient techniques but only as if the patients could have saved everybody time and effort by not getting into trouble again. Pressed, the staff might well admit that hemophiliac individuals cannot do much to prevent these frequent crises, but. . . . A detached observer might be inclined to say that this routine kind of rescue work probably should be going on elsewhere than in a big medical center, presumably at some medical facility where the staff does not define its work either as curing or as the immensely specialized management of acute disease.

To the foregoing discussion of crisis prevention and crisis management, it should also be added that *during* an extended period of crisis (whether the patient is in the hospital or at home) some organization of family effort is still called for. The kinsmen may need to make special arrangements about their time (from work, for visiting the hospital, for nursing the patient at home). They may also need to make arrangements about space (having the bed downstairs rather than upstairs, living near the hospital during the peak of the crisis). They may have to juggle the immediate and even the extended family's finances. They may have to spell each other, in an extraordinary division of family labor, when taking care of the patient at home during his crisis. Even the patient—in trying "to get better" rather than "giving up" or in acting properly rather than tempting fate by improper actions—may have to contribute to the organization of effort necessary to bringing him (and his kinsmen) through his period of danger.

REFERENCES

1. Kesten, Yehuda: Diary of a heart patient, New York, 1968, McGraw-Hill Book Co.
2. Lenneberg, E., and Rowbotham, J.: The ileostomy patient, Springfield, Illinois, 1970, Charles C Thomas, Publisher.
3. Massie, Robert: Nicholas and Alexandra, New York, 1967, Dell Publishing Co., Inc.
4. *San Francisco Chronicle*, April 10, 1971, © Chronicle Publishing Co., 1971.
5. *San Francisco Chronicle*, November 5, 1971. Story reprinted from a United Press International Release.

CHAPTER 2

MANAGEMENT OF REGIMENS

A second key problem encountered by many, if not most, of the chronically ill is the management of their regimens, for unless the physician is absolutely helpless in the face of a given chronic disease, he will suggest or command some kind of regimen. At first blush, regimen management may not seem a problem of much magnitude: regimens are either followed by obedient, sensible patients or ignored at their peril. Indeed, physicians and other health personnel tend to regard patients (or their families) as not only foolish if they do not carry out the prescribed regimens but as downright uncooperative. They talk approvingly or disapprovingly about the adherence or lack of adherence to regimens. It is true that sometimes patients and families foolishly and even willfully break the rules, as when the mother of a child allergic to chocolate allows him "just one piece."

However, the issue is not really one of willfullness, stupidity, or even medical ignorance. The issue is primarily that patients must continue to manage their daily existences under specific sets of financial and social conditions. Their chronic illnesses and the associated regimens only complicate—and are secondary to—their daily management problems. In that regard, regimens sometimes present even more difficulties than the symptoms themselves. It is no wonder, then, that every regimen—and every item in it—is actually or potentially on trial. So are the people who recommend the regimen.

REGIMENS ARE EVALUATED

Regimens, then, are *not* just automatically accepted. They are judged either on the basis of efficiency or legitimacy or both. Also, they are judged on social rather than medical bases. Hence, they will be taken up and adhered to only under certain conditions. Some of these are:

1. There is an initial or continuing trust in the physician or whoever else prescribes the regimen.
2. No rival supercedes the physician in his legitimating.
3. There is evidence that the regimen works either to control symptoms or the disease itself or both.
4. No distressing, frightening side effects appear.

5. The side effects are outweighed by symptom relief or by sufficient fear of the disease itself.
6. There is a relative noninterference with important daily activities, either of the patient or of people around him.
7. The regimen's perceived good effects are not outweighed by a negative impact on the patient's sense of identity.

Such evaluations are not just made once and for all but are made continually if not continuously! We shall see some of these conditions for evaluation at work below.

REGIMENS HAVE CHARACTERISTICS
Learning the regimen

After an initial acceptance of the regimen—whether prescribed by a doctor, chiropractor, osteopath, naturopath, or someone else—the most important chronological event is that the patient (or parent or wife, if need be) learns how to administer the regimen. Regimens, of course, can have various characteristics, but two vis-à-vis learning are very important: whether they entail eliminating something (food, activities) or adding something (drugs, activities). Some additions or eliminations are very easy to learn. Some, however, involve procedures that can be difficult, especially at first, such as giving asthma shots or monitoring body wastes.

When the regimen involves a machine, as in kidney dialysis, the learning can be quite a complex matter—and then the relevant health personnel are more likely to take the time to teach the patient or his kinsmen what they need to know. Even with such a crucial regimen, however, there can be organizational "slips," as one social scientist who was working as an experienced technician on a dialysis unit has written:

> On another occasion, I took a telephone call from a patient who had been home a week and had just finished rebuilding his first Kiil. He wanted to know how to fill it with formaldehyde to sterilize it, saying he didn't remember the precise procedure. I answered his questions and mentioned to the evening staff later that he had called. Their reactions were surprising. He had been taught the procedure . . . and his calling the center was simply the usual psychological reaction of patients who had just been sent home. The patient just wanted someone in the center to talk to and reassure him that he had not been abandoned. I tried to point out that while the method for sterilizing Kiil is simple, actually carrying out the steps can be confusing unless one had done it several times, and that furthermore this patient had been trained during the days and that evening staff had no way of knowing what had or had not been taught. Staff was adamant, however, and replied that I "had been in dialysis long enough to know better."[1]

Learning how to carry out the regimen can, at first, be very anxiety provoking.

> At the initial session of learning how to give insulin shots, the mother of a diabetic child shook so much that she dropped the needle and burst into tears. *Benoliel*

When life may hang on proper carrying out of a regimen through machinery, then anxiety may be almost unbearable during the early phases of learning to use and live with the machine.

> One family, whose child had cystic fibrosis, remarked that they no longer went out at night. ("I don't even trust my sister to do the right things.") Both parents were so acutely anxious about the mist-tent pump and the possibility of its going bad that they constantly listened for any change in noise or rhythm and also constantly checked the water bottle to make certain it was not empty.   *Benoliel*

Sometimes the regimens are not easy for the patient or his assisting kinsmen to learn.

> Mrs. F. said sometimes she just hated to go see Dr. Y. because Johnnie wasn't coughing productively. She thought the physical therapist really wanted to wash her hands of them. It is only since Johnnie's last hospitalization, a month ago, that he learned to cough productively, and to bring up large amounts of mucus.
> *Benoliel*

Difficulties in learning regimens may not, however, result solely from the complexity of procedures or the accompanying anxiety, but also from the regimen's impact on personal identity. It is one thing for a person with cardiac disease to be told "walk," another for one with diabetes (and his agents) to hear that he must stay *for life* on that regimen! Being on a dermatological regimen that involves smearing a large portion of one's body with disgusting looking ointment can be quite devastating. To be hooked into the frequent use of machinery—whether it be life-saving, like a dialysis machine, or as innocuous as a bronchial inhalator—can be profoundly disturbing, if only because one feels a slave to the machinery. Identities are challenged, too, by the requirement of "staying with" the regimen: if one cannot meet the challenge (quite like fat people who are ordered onto a dietary regimen), then one may feel characterless, a genuine failure. Control agents who cannot keep their ill children or husbands on necessary regimens can easily blame themselves, not merely their sick charges, especially when they have been somewhat lax in their efforts at control or if, regardless, the illness worsens.

Time and regimen

Various other characteristics of a regimen may call for considerable organization of personal or family effort. Consider the matter of time. Some regimens take many minutes or even hours to carry out. This means that the requisite time must be available, otherwise the regimen will be omitted or at least altered so as to be of shorter duration. Some regimens must be done twice or three times daily; this activity may run counter to working steadily on the job or interfere with very busy weekends. Some regimens must be carried out on schedule or timed in relation to the peaking of symptoms, rather than flexibly altered to fit whatever time is available.

People who have had colostomy operations often schedule their movements in accordance to the scheduling of their irrigations, which must be done at home. Their mobility, therefore, tends to be restricted to the distance that can be covered in the time between irrigations. Their sociability away from home, indeed their social contacts, are "limited to periods between irrigations." In other words, they are of rather short duration unless occurring at home. "Patients can, therefore, be considered as living 'on a leash' which is only as long as the time interval between irrigations."[2]

Regimens may even occupy so much time (entire days on a kidney dialysis machine) that they are virtually at the center of a person's life. On the other hand, time may be a relatively minor problem even when the regimen must be carried out with frequency. Thus even when pills must be taken often, pill-popping does not take much time. Likewise, sometimes duration is easily managed: patients can listen to music, or think, or even do business work while engaging in lengthy regimen procedures. When the treatment involves going to a health facility, where waiting time is added to regimen time, then patients find it more difficult to plan their daily time exactly, though they may utilize the waiting time to read, knit, or whatever.

Discomfort, effort, energy, and visibility

Another characteristic of regimens is the amount of discomfort they cause. The discomfort can be direct, as with the pain caused by some physiotherapy exercises. The discomfort can also involve side effects, like indigestion or dizziness or lethargy induced by drugs. When, in addition, the side effects signify danger or risk to the person or his family, he is much less inclined to continue the regimen unaltered unless it signifies less risk than does his continuing with the present symptoms or having his disease unchecked. Thus people with chronic bronchitis will cut down on their postural drainage, skipping or shortening the sessions, at least until their symptoms become quite bothersome or alarming.

Another characteristic of the regimen is the amount of effort or energy it takes to complete it in its prescribed form. This implies not merely time consumed but quite literally the sufficient energy and effort that must be mustered up for the task. (Emphysema patients who simply do not have enough energy to climb the stairs to their second and third floor apartments will leave breathing equipment untouched during the day.) If someone is ill or tired, he is that much less likely to be able or want to carry out the regimen. If, in addition, carrying out the regimen requires the assistance of another person, as with cystic fibrosis exercises, then both need to have sufficient energy to do the job. If, for example, the mother has been ill and cannot muster up sufficient energy or if the child is tired and does not wish to put out the required effort, then the exercise is much more likely to be skipped.

Another characteristic of the regimen is whether or not it is visible to other people and what that visibility means to the patient. If the visible regimen means that a stigmatized disease can be suspected or discovered, the person is most unlikely to carry out the regimen in public. Yet, the physician's orders may require that he do it sufficiently so that it *is* public. (Patients with tuberculosis sometimes have to cope with this problem.) If the visible regimen is no more than slightly embarrassing or is fully explainable, then its visibility is much less likely to prevent its public occurrence. If its visibility is partly reduced, as when someone disappears fairly frequently to the bathroom even though everyone notices how often he must go, the regimen will probably be followed.

Efficiency

Another characteristic is also important: if the regimen is "readable" as efficient ("it works") by the patient, then that *may* convince him that he should continue with it. But continuance is problematic, not only because other properties already noted may counteract his best intentions or his good sense, but because an effective regimen may mean to him that now it is time to go off it—no matter what the physician says. This is exactly what happens when patients with tuberculosis see their symptoms disappear and figure that now they can cut out—partially or totally—their discomforting regimen of massive pill swallowing.

> That this is not an unusual act is illustrated by the story of one patient who had slight back pains, and so went to a physician who diagnosed the pain and gave him a relaxant drug, but then cut down and finally ceased taking the drug as soon as the pains totally disappeared. He was only unusual in that he told his physician—who was startled at the open revelation.

Also relevant to the seeming efficiency of a regimen is the speed with which its efficiency is displayed to the patient. To continue with a treatment, as in cancer, that does not have rather immediate results, but, indeed, sometimes just the reverse, takes quite a bit of fear of the disease itself and trust in the physician. If pain or discomfort (physiotherapy) or the elimination of favorite foods is added to the slowness with which efficiency is demonstrated, then it takes much trust in the physician or real fear of the disease or great desire to be rid of the symptoms to carry out the regimen.

Denial and confusion

The very characteristics of the regimen, then, constitute important contributing conditions for adhering to, relaxing, or even rejecting the prescribed regimen. A few other important conditions are worth mentioning. Thus if the patient simply denies that he has the disease, he may refuse to submit to a regimen or may only minimally carry it out. (As with tuberculosis, many patients actually experience no symptoms and will not take the physician's reading of the ambiguous—to them—x-ray signs as proof of illness.) Again, a patient may wish very much to adhere to a regimen but the instructions about it leave him confused or baffled. For instance, cardiac patients told to "rest" can be much frustrated because they do not really know of what sufficient rest consists. Being told to "find your own limits" is no great help either, although it does give tacit permission to experiment with an unavoidably flexible regimen.

Expense

A very important additional characteristic of regimens is the expense for the patient, especially where drugs or machinery are involved. Patients are more likely to cut back on drug regimens if they are expensive, especially when their efficiency is not speedily demonstrated or where they bring about discomfort.

> The parents of a child with asthma were discouraged with the lack of response to treatments in light, especially of their expensiveness. They remarked that these had been costly—and it wouldn't be so bad if there were some positive results— but there's no improvement. It had been a difficult year financially; hospitalization was $400, only half covered by insurance, and none of the doctor's bills were covered; also there were bills for medicine, inhalators, and so on.   *Benoliel*

If, however, the disease is very dangerous, patients are more likely to give funding for the regimen considerable priority over their spending for other activities and objects.

In general, however, funding problems do affect whether and to what extent the regimen is followed. Thus emphysema patients with little money who are not supposed to climb stairs cannot easily choose to move to a more expensive first floor apartment, giving up their rather cheap third-story rent. The result is they do not use their breathing machines because they would have to go upstairs to use them when once downstairs. Another consideration is that if a regimen—as with drugs—involves a considerable amount of money and yet does not seem to be rather quickly affecting either the symptoms or the disease itself, then there is apt to be at least some cutback on the amount of drug taking. The balancing here is between the cost of the regimen and its evaluated efficiency.

Isolation and comprehension

Yet another condition for nonadherence or partial adherence is that the regimen leads increasingly to social isolation, so that the patient has to decide whether the regimen's effects are worth the loss of sociability and human contact.

There is one final condition: if the patient and/or kinsmen do not have a very accurate view of the deterioration accompanying the disease, then they are that less likely to stick with an otherwise difficult, discomforting, or time-consuming regimen. Immediate deterioration or occasionally severe crises would counteract that tendency to relax or abandon the regimen; but in their absence, only some view (even if dead wrong) of deleterious results may prevent relaxation or abandonment of the regimen. This kind of medical ignorance sometimes results from inadequate communication between physician and patient—either because the professional does not take time to explain or is not skilled at explaining, or because the lay person may not understand the technical language of the physician. Of course, sometimes the patient does not wish to hear.

Summary

Now that we have reviewed a substantial number of regimen characteristics, we shall actually list them. This is worth doing in order to emphasize, as if underlined in red, that the view of a patient's breaking the regimen (foolish, ignorant, obstinate) that is all too often held by health personnel is just too simplistic, too stereotyped. Just scanning the list is likely to make one wonder at how anyone (including himself) manages to stay with his regimen, even in modified form!

1. Is difficult or easy to learn and to carry out.
2. Takes much or little time.
3. Causes much or little discomfort or pain.
4. Does or does not cause side effects, especially if they are actually or seemingly risky ones.
5. Needs much or little effort or energy to carry out.
6. Is or is not visible to others.
7. If known, might or might not cause others to stigmatize the person.
8. Does or does not seem efficient.
9. Is or is not expensive.
10. Does or does not lead to increasing social isolation.

To make the issue of adherence or nonadherence even more graphic, we might consider the following diagram. It involves the ideas that a *regimen* can be (1) easy, (2) difficult, or (3) very difficult; that the patient's *life-style* can be (1) much affected, (2) somewhat affected, or (3) very little affected by the regimen; and that the *disease or the symptoms* may be (1) minimally or (2) maximally affected by the regimen (as the patient sees it). Now, imagine how likely, or unlikely, a patient is to follow a regimen faithfully when it falls into any of the various situations pictured in the diagram. Certainly the two extreme cases (A and B) are, respectively, the least likely and the most likely to be followed exactly.

LIFE-STYLE

Disease or symptom	Much affected		Somewhat affected		Little affected	
	MINIMAL	MAXIMAL	MINIMAL	MAXIMAL	MINIMAL	MAXIMAL
Easy regimen						B
Difficult regimen						
Very difficult regimen	A					

AGENTS: COOPERATING AND CONFLICTING

If a person does choose to stick by his regimen, this will require some degree of personal and often familial organization of effort. We shall not develop this point very much, since it was a feature of the earlier discussion of crises. It is worth mentioning, however, that there are at least two principal kinds of agents. One is the assisting agent, as with the parent who helps the child with his cystic fibrosis breathing exercises. The second is the control agent, who helps the tempted or recalcitrant patient stick to his regimen, using various tactics like issuing commands or manipulating indirectly ("I always take a little away from his lunch and evening meals to allow for snacking—such as popcorn at the movies"). Additional tactics include shaming and reminding. When the agent fails to do his part of the cooperative job, then the regimen is not likely to be implemented, or at least not effectively. The agent can be tired, ill, uninterested, or disbelieve in the regimen.

The control agent may also not be able to get, or at least maintain, control if the ill person "has a mind of his or her own." In such instances, sometimes not even a kinsman is instituting influence or restraint but someone else. Thus, a friend of mine who was dying of cancer:

> runs her own show, with her mother as the assisting agent but not a control agent. Today Fran took specially cooked food over to Helen. Helen was about to have hamburger, but Fran put her foot down—that's not the thing to eat after yesterday's and today's bouts of diarrhea. "Can I eat your food?" Helen asks, and Fran says "yes" and explains why. Then Helen asks her mother for a glass of wine. Fran says that makes no sense. Helen then gets angry at her mother because she'd been allowing her to drink wine! In effect, Helen has never allowed her mother to be much of a control agent. Fran was able to, because accidentally she entered the act at the right time: if she'd insisted on "no wine" earlier—or maybe later—she'd have lost the argument too. Fran did feel badly in denying Helen the wine: she's not experienced at such controlling!

Also, two people in the family can disagree about a regimen such as when the father believes it ridiculous or ineffective, but the mother believes the physician. Such domestic disagreement, and even overt conflict, will certainly affect whether and how much the regimen is followed.

Where there is cooperation in the family, there is often a division of labor.

> Mr. V. doesn't participate in the coughing procedures of his son with cystic fibrosis because he doesn't have the patience to "work with" the child, coaxing, encouraging, and waiting. But he does help with the child's special tent and bed. The mother believes that if the husband didn't share the work that way, she could not live with the burden of her sick child.   *Benoliel*

Domestic division of labor can also be much affected by relationships within the family.

> In another family affected by cystic fibrosis, both parents help with the exercises and treatments, but the husband does more because he has more authority. The

mother has difficulty getting the child to do the difficult regimen without accompanying big scenes.   *Benoliel*

Sometimes the entire family may be "in on the act" of aiding, assisting, or controlling the patient. Thus, a diabetic individual can maintain his diet if everyone in the family follows *his* diet. More implicitly, if an asthmatic mother is advised to "get rid" of her child's dog, then the child, too, is participating in her elimination regimen. But siblings may occasionally rebel: "Everything has to be done for old Louise!"

The physician and other health personnel may, of course, also act as assisting agents (physical therapists, for example) or control agents. They may persuade and dissuade when they believe it necessary. They may do this with great tact or, alas, not always so nicely—though admittedly, impoliteness and threat sometimes bring results. The two extremes:

> The physician talked to the child about giving up eating wheat, saying this was difficult but really he thought wheat was the problem and would he give it a try. He talked about his own allergy to grapes and having to give up drinking wine. Would Jim give it a try? Jim agreed and they shook hands.   *Benoliel*

> After a kidney transplant and refusal to follow the regimen, his kidney (in an examination at the clinic) shows signs of being rejected. He makes a big scene, when told, cursing physicians and yelling that he wasn't being helped. He refuses to be hospitalized. His main physician was out of town, but when phoned told his nurse to say: "Well, Joe, if you want to commit suicide, just stay at home and don't bother us any more. We're trying to help you, but you don't want it." *Suczek*

Sometimes there is considerable misunderstanding between the physician or other health personnel and the person concerning the terms of his regimen. Even where the instructions are simple and extremely important—as in the number of pills a transplant patient should take—the patient may not hear correctly. Besides simple mishearing, conditions for misunderstanding include the health personnel's unawareness of situations which may lead to "rule breaking"—specific home conditions, domestic conditions, and cultural values (as toward specific foods which are highly esteemed or tabooed). In addition, the physician may just be thoughtless or unrealistic, as was a pediatrician who put a young child on 85 units of insulin four times daily—the last dose at midnight: the mother commented caustically: "Can you imagine waking a kid up at midnight for that!"

When the regimen requires really professional skill and is a matter of life and death, then understandably the patient is called into the hospital where the treatment given him is, in fact, just another form of regimen. Out of danger, or taught the requisite skills, he can be sent home; or if need be, as with radiation therapy for cancer, he must return at intervals to have his regimen carried out by the professionals.

Given the exigencies of life and the changing patterns of symptoms, inevitably patients and kinsmen enter into negotiations with each other, and sometimes with health personnel, over relaxing or otherwise changing the regimen (substituting one drug for another, one activity for another). They are negotiating not merely over such matters as the elimination of discomfort and side effects, but over the much more primary issue of how the management of ordinary life can be made easier or even possible. Health personnel, of course, recognize much of this bargaining and sympathize with it if the stakes seem reasonable. What they do not always recognize is just how high the stakes may be for the patient and his family. They ignore those to the peril of their mutual relationships: at worst, the patient may go shopping for another doctor and other help; at the least, he may quietly alter his regimen or substitute or supplement it with something drawn from another source (a pharmacist, a friend, an aunt).

> A Chinese-American health professional with asthmatic attacks has chest specialists who, out of professional courtesy and colleagueship, checked on him at frequent intervals. He understood his medications and all the implications. Since the attacks robbed him of sleep and energy and severe attacks were unpredictable, he was ready to try anything that might work. He consulted two herbalists, took his medications and herbs concurrently. . . .[3]

ADHERING TO AND MODIFYING THE REGIMEN

It should now be evident that sick people do not necessarily regard all elements of a regimen as having equal priority. They may strictly follow some elements but slack off or totally reject other elements, for instance, those that give indigestion or seem not to be working. Patients may do this after bargaining with the physician or they simply may not tell him about their modifications of the prescribed regimen. Moreover, other persons may act to dissuade them from following certain parts of the regimen, or indeed all of it, and even persuade them to try alternative regimens. About the latter, they often give testimonials drawn from their own experience or based on hearsay.

Patients also shop around for alternatives, either because a current regimen does not seem to be working well or because there ought to be a better one, or at least one that works faster, is less uncomfortable, demands less effort, or is less costly. On the other hand, if life is at stake and there is considerable trust in the physician, then the ill person is likely to consider that the entire regimen is binding. Not to carry it out is to court disaster and quite possibly death. As one person on dialysis said with finality: "It's going to be done and that's it!" And another:

> It's taken me a long while to adjust. Before, especially the day before I come in, I don't want to go. There's the boredom of lying here all day, and some pain. Then I think, "You don't go, you're going to die!" and I force myself to adjust.   *Suczek*

The organization of effort necessary for carrying out some regimens not only has to be instituted and maintained, it requires the "learning through experience" of everything that must go into juggling life while carrying out the regimen. So, one has to learn what are his own, unique reactions to various aspects of his regimen—and how to handle daily living in the face of those reactions. He has to learn how much of the regimen will handle how much of his symptoms, and whether he wants more or less of those symptoms controlled—in terms of the impact on his daily living. He has to learn, too, what differences carrying out his regimen will make in relationships with his kinsmen, friends, acquaintances, fellow employees, supervisors, or employers. All the foregoing amounts to learning what difference his regimen is making—right now—in his and their style and quality of life. Thus, along with learning to institute and maintain personal-familial effort that will support the implementation of a regimen goes their respective learning to organize the wider realm of maintaining as much of a normal life as seems possible in the face of needing to control the symptoms or the disease itself.

If the course of the disease and its symptoms are not sufficiently held in check by the regimen, so that they all impact drastically on his life, then the patient inevitably will begin to think about whether it is all worth the price. He will be balancing life against death. Again a quotation from a dialysis patient, this one with only a couple of months of experience behind her:

> In the beginning, it's as if that machine is a human being with a brain and it's *running* you. Then you realize it is only a machine and the brain is *yours*. Then you are suddenly faced with the fact that you're very nearly at death's door and you have to depend on that machine to stay alive—*that's* upsetting. The question at that point is why bother? Why go to all this bother just to stay alive? It takes time to get your evaluations going and to know just where you're going. *Suczek*

Some dialysis patients, of course, do choose death. They go off the machine; or, if stopped from doing that, they outwit their physicians and their families by some other method of ending their lives, as in the instance of a young man who, alone for 10 minutes, pulled out his shunt and bled to death. However sad such a story is, we can still understand and empathize with the choice. Harder still on the bystanders, kinsmen, and health personnel alike is an election to die. In the words of the researcher:

> Johnnie was dying but slowly. In recent weeks, he had refused to do his postural drainage, and his mother had finally gone along with him. He has become progressively morose, and his mother has told the physician she couldn't stand it because he never smiled anymore. The physician thinks perhaps she feels guilty about having forced the treatment on Johnnie, and also for wanting him now to die. *Benoliel*

When likable children elect to die more quickly than they might, the health personnel can also be terribly upset, especially when they have known them before and have become very attached to them.

Let us return, however, to the more usual and happier cases where ill persons are trying to maintain relatively normal lives—a task that can only be controlled by the patient and/or his agents. It neither belongs to the health personnel nor can it be delegated to them, except during medical crises. They can only help in its solution if they are aware of its possible complexity. Every deleterious change in symptomatology, every item added to the regimen, every shift of social relationships in which the person is engaged will alter his and his family's task of organizing their lives satisfactorily, despite the symptoms *and* the regimen.

MULTIPLE DISEASES AND THEIR REGIMENS

Many people suffer from more than one chronic illness. This means they may be simultaneously on two or three or more regimens. To carry out each may take considerable juggling of time and effort. It is easy to see that some regimens may suffer in favor of others. Peak periods of danger or of bothersome symptoms will give priority to the corresponding regimens. What is not as obvious is that certain regimens may actually exacerbate the symptoms of another illness.

> Mr. Smith has both chronic bronchitis and a stomach hernia. For the first, he is supposed to do several minutes of daily postural drainage. But this enhances the probability that he will get heartburn from his hernia. Furthermore, if he attempts to reduce the probability of his hernial heartburn by using a high pillow while sleeping, that sometimes brings on pains, ordinarily quiescent, from a pinched neck nerve.

Patients may not always be thoroughly rational in how they decide among competing regimens, but decide they must. The choice is not necessarily as their physician would advise, if he knew—but the choice is theirs, not his!

SUPPLEMENTING AND SHOPPING AROUND

From much of the foregoing discussion, it can easily be seen that even when a patient thoroughly trusts his physician, he does not necessarily follow *only* the physician's instructions or commands. He may very well supplement those with additional regimen items learned, or searched out, elsewhere.

A study of how the Chinese and American-born Chinese in San Francisco utilize health services demonstrates that ill persons may supplement physician regimens with herbs recommended by a herbalist, the services of an acupuncturist, or foods and other items including drugs recommended by kinsmen and neighbors.[3] Understandably, those who are more chronically ill tend to be receptive to multiple sources of regimens. While non-Chinese usually do not have herbalists' counsel to draw upon, they freely utilize the services of chiropractors, osteopaths, faith healers, and many other types of seemingly knowledgeable or experienced persons. They use their advice not only in lieu of but in addition to that of licensed physicians. Furthermore, when a doctor's regimen does not seem to be working efficiently or rapidly, they will eventually search out another physician or another type of healer and switch to him.

From the standpoint of the physicians, switching tends to reflect either an unjustifiable lack of faith or, in the case of patients with fatal diseases, search for the impossible cure. From the standpoint of the sick person, the physician is simply the source of necessary services: among those services are the ones pertaining to regimens—what to do, what not to do, and access to the drugs, machinery, or procedure essential to the carrying out of the regimens. In short, to understand why patients switch, supplement, or at least only partly adhere to the physician's regimen, we must understand that his regimen or counsel does not stand alone but is only an element in a complicated pattern of living.

REFERENCES

1. Chu, George: The kidney patient: a socio-medical study, Ph.D. thesis, School of Public Health, University of California, Berkeley, 1975.
2. Goffman, Erving: Stigma, Englewood Cliffs, New Jersey, 1963, Prentice-Hall, Inc., p. 91. Goffman is quoting from Orbach, C., Bard, M., and Sutherland, A.: Fears and defensive adaptations to the loss of sphincter control, Psychoanalytic Review 44:121-175, 1957.
3. Louie, Theresa: The pragmatic context: a Chinese-American example of defining and managing illness, Ph.D. thesis, School of Nursing, University of California, San Francisco, 1975.

CHAPTER 3

SYMPTOM CONTROL

The control of symptoms is so obviously linked with adherence to effective regimens that, having seen the complexity of that phenomenon, we are not likely to conceive of symptom control as merely a matter of medical management. Of course, the correct choice of regimens can be crucial for both disease and symptom control, and during medical crises the wisdom and care of the professionals may be absolutely essential. Yet the sick person spends most of the time away from the medical facilities, so he and his family must rely upon their own judgment, wisdom, and ingenuity for controlling his symptoms.

A portion of that need for judgment, wisdom, and ingenuity is recognized by health personnel—but probably only a small portion. Physicians, of course, do indicate to a patient (with respect to certain diseases) that he must work out aspects of regimen—like how woozy he gets from a given amount of drug—and also discover the idiosyncrasies of his own body to better control symptoms. But to a great degree, the sick person is on his own insofar as he requires an intense awareness of his body: what it can and cannot do *now*, as opposed to before. Of course, people with lifelong illnesses, and especially those who have no great ups and downs in symptomatology, have long since come to terms with their bodies, managing their symptoms with relative skill and sometimes with scarcely any awareness of management because they are just part of their daily life. But with newly appearing diseases or symptoms, a person may discover that his body is a very surprising thing indeed. He will need to come to terms with it and develop new relationships with it. Thus, a cardiac patient who now suffers from sudden losses of energy simply cannot ignore his changed body. The "cannot ignore" probably will involve coping not only with something physically new but with something affecting one's sense of self:

> Richie, a stroke patient, has described how when awakening from sleep with a pain in his right side, he would carefully have to think through what to do. He would seize his upper right arm with his left hand, prying loose his right arm and hand "from wherever they had got to be—I usually was sitting on my right hand. . . ." He felt that both his right arm and leg "behaved like strangers . . .

the absence of touch was psychologically important. It meant that the limbs did not belong to me."[7]

How drastic the changes and the requisite adaptations can be is poignantly illustrated by the extraordinary movements of a patient with myasthenia gravis who had great muscular flaccidity. In the words of the research nurse who interviewed him at home:

> He lifted his pills into his mouth by using the sides of both his hands, and he lifted the cup by encircling his palms about it and lifting it to his mouth. This was not an easy operation for him. . . . As we talked he struggled to assume relaxed, conversational postures which he was not able to hold for more than a few seconds. His most comfortable position seemed to be one of having his arms resting and outstretched on the table. If he tried to bend his arms up from the elbow with the elbows on the table, in a moment or two the arms would fall down. He tried to cross his arms across his chest or cross his arms or rest the elbows on the table; but they would simply fall.   *Davis*

Whatever sophisticated technical references there may be for his symptoms, the person who has symptoms will be concerned primarily with whether he hurts, faints, trembles visibly, loses energy suddenly, runs short of breath, has had his mobility or his speech impaired, or is evidencing some kind of disfigurement. Aside from what these may signify to him about his disease or his life-span, such symptoms can interfere with his life and his social relationships. How much they interfere depends on whether they are permanent or temporary, frequent or occasional, predictable or unpredictable, and publicly visible or invisible; upon their degree (as of pain), their meaning to bystanders (as of disfigurement), and the nature of the regimen called for to control the symptom; and upon the kinds of life-style and social relations that the sufferer has hitherto sustained.

REDESIGNING LIFE-STYLES

Even minor, occasional symptoms may lead to some changing of habits. Thus someone who begins to suffer from minor back pains is likely to learn to avoid certain kinds of chairs and even discover, to his dismay, that a favorite sitting position is precisely what he must eliminate from his repertoire. Major symptoms, however, may call for the redesigning or reshaping of important aspects of a life-style. Thus the stroke patient quoted earlier has also written that:

> Before you come downstairs, stop and think. Handkerchief, money, keys, book, and so on—if you come downstairs without these, you will have to climb upstairs, or send someone to get them.[7]

People with chronic diarrhea need to reshape their conventional habits like this:

> I never go to local movies. If I go . . . I select a large house . . . where I have a greater choice of seats. . . . When I go on a bus . . . I sit on an end seat or near the door.[2]

Major redesigning can involve moving to a one-story house, buying clothes that cloak disfigurement, getting the boss to assign jobs that require less strength, and using crutches or other aids to mobility. Some of the alternative possibilities are more unusual; they are based on the ingenuity of the sufferer or on his stumbling on a solution. The case studies, in Part Two, on colitis and on emphysema are especially replete with examples of ingenuity through necessity—or desperation—like the mailman who lived "on a leash," having arranged never to be very far from that necessary toilet while on his job, or the emphysema sufferers who learn to use "puffing stations," where they can recoup from lack of breath while looking as if their stopping were normal.

In working out this redesigning of activities, friends, kinsmen, and health personnel may also provide the truly effective or inventive idea. (They are redesigning agents.) Some examples: a community nurse taught an emphysema patient how to rest while doing his household chores. A woman, in the absence of attentive personnel, taught her sister (afflicted with brittle bones because of a destructive drug) how to get up from the toilet, without a back brace, without breaking bones in her back. Another woman figured out how her cardiac-arthritic grandfather could continue his beloved walks on his farm by placing wooden stumps at short distances, so that he could rest as he reached each one. Unfortunately, relatives and health personnel can function in just the opposite fashion. For instance, a woman with multiple sclerosis had carefully arranged her one-room apartment so that literally every object she needed was within arm's reach. But the public health nurse who visited her regarded the place as in a terrible shambles, urged less disorder, and proceeded to tidy up things a bit herself.

Some people are very inventive in what we may term "devising," that is, working out physical arrangements that permit them to do things without undue discomfort or pain or drain on energy. Many arthritic individuals are very clever at devising to accommodate their partly disabled hands and feet. They find and use old-fashioned collar-button hooks in order to manage their otherwise recalcitrant buttons. (One stroke patient scoured the city of New York looking for an instrument that would solve the frustrating problem of managing his shirt buttons. He remarks caustically: "The doctors were at their blandest and most maddening here: not only did they have no solution, they pretended there was no problem."[5]) They also buy clothes with zippers instead of struggling with buttons. They fix faucets so they can be moved with elbows. Arthritic people with bad feet or cardiac sufferers who have little energy for mounting stairs too frequently make certain that two sets of eyeglasses and other objects in daily use are distributed upstairs and downstairs. People with low energy may devise ways, too, to avoid pushing open the heavy entry doors of public buildings, including hospitals, for example, by falling into step behind people with more normal reserves of energy.

Perhaps the lack of inventiveness and social skills—quite as much as poor finances or few material resources—are what prevent people from not reaching some relatively satisfying redesign of life. The cancer patient with lessened energy who can ingeniously juggle her friends' visits and telephone calls can manage to sustain a relatively unimpaired social life. The arthritic farm ladies who can make arrangements with neighbors to bring in the store groceries can live on their farms during the summer, although they must move to town for the winter months.

> One sufferer of multiple sclerosis of our acquaintance (a student) not only has rearranged her apartment but has persuaded various people to do various things necessary because of her increasingly restricted mobility; she has had a veritable army of people come to her aid—the University architect redesigned certain of the public toilets for her wheelchair and also put in some ramps; the handymen around the University help her up and down stairs daily, by appointment; they have also rebuilt her cupboards so that they are reachable from her wheelchair; and so on.

It is certainly worth adding—and emphasizing—that among those who are most advantageously placed to help as skilled redesigning or devising agents are the health personnel. They are apt to meet a great number of patients—say, those with arthritis—who share virtually identical symptoms necessitating redesigning strategies. If personnel are alert to how those patients have handled their problems, they might pass along very helpful information to each new patient. "You know, I talked with someone last week, Mrs. Jones, who. . . ." Alas, how many health personnel know neither what Mrs. Jones did nor what Mrs. Smith needs; and how many, even when knowledgeable, bother to communicate their knowledge? In our view, all health personnel should regard themselves as conduits through which such information flows from one inventive sick person to another. They should be active transmitters of that information, that is, intelligent transmitting agents!

FAILURE AT REDESIGNING

When the sufferer or his agents are unable to figure out how to ease or get around his symptom, or to have it discounted through some social arrangement, then he will have to pay for his failure. Sometimes he pays physically, sometimes socially. It is worth noting that the making of new or different social arrangements may not simply be a matter of intelligent solution or social skill but may be affected by moral considerations. Some patients with multiple sclerosis would not have been able to do what the student did because they would have seen her activities as taking undue advantage of strangers or as showing a lack of pride in oneself. Certainly the social isolation attending multiple sclerosis[1] is contributed to by the lack of social skills and by the personal pride, but also by some failure of ingenuity by the ill persons, their family members, and friends.

Good solutions are also a matter of good fortune in having skillful or inventive friends and relatives who can help with the reshaping and reformation of social relationships pertinent to the management of one's symptoms. If, however, they choose to oppose one's own ideas for rearrangements, that can make symptom control more difficult. The situation is especially difficult, sometimes, when the rearrangement of others' lives is also involved. Thus an asthmatic woman said:

> Some of my friends simply don't understand that I am allergic to animals. They are so fond of them, they get upset that I can't have them about, and really don't believe me. They are so sensitive about their animals.

She also remarked that:

> My friends now understand that during my worst periods I can't come to their homes unless the dust is minimized. So they will clean the day before I visit, and I'll wait for the dust to settle before going there.

Even when other people do not oppose the chronically ill person's ideas about redesigning but simply show poor judgment or lack of imagination about useful redesigning, symptom control is made additionally difficult. The point is illustrated on a large institutional scale by the relative lack of imagination in the redesigning of homes for the elderly, as anyone can attest if he watches these stiff-jointed or low-energied people either as they struggle to rise from sitting positions on low sofas and chairs or as they carefully pick their way along highly polished corridors—without handrails.

INTERACTIONAL CONSIDERATIONS

The reshaping of activities pertains not only to items of life-style but, because of the potential or actual visibility of symptoms, to the crucial issue of interaction. There is need for a variety of judicious or clever maneuvers in order to keep one's symptoms as little intrusive as possible—to hide them, disguise them, minimize them, temporarily eliminate them, or at least help to change their public meaning.

Sometimes the tactics are very simple: a college teacher with bronchitis, whose peak load of coughing up sputum is in the morning, arranges his teaching schedule so that he can stay at home, or at least in his office, until after lunchtime. Another person, who tends continually to have a runny allergic nose, always carries tissue in her hand when in public so that she does not call more attention to herself by rummaging in her pocketbook for it. Another with a tendency to cough carries cough drops with him—especially requisite when he attends concerts. More difficult problems can arise. If someone cannot help coughing up sputum in public, then he is careful not to allow the offensive matter to show by completely covering his mouth with the tissue. And anyone who coughs much will need to explain persuasively or indicate that his cough is not infectious! An epileptic man or woman may have to persuade acquaintances that epileptic fits are not communicative! Emphysema sufferers learn to sit down or lean against buildings in such a fashion that they are not mistaken for drunks or bring themselves to embarrassing public attention. People with heart trouble need to explain that when they feel it necessary to lie down, that signifies merely a draining of energy and not that they are having another heart attack! The need for rather continual monitoring of symptoms—and so for more complex interactional tactics still—is illustrated vividly by the case study on colitis, where we see colitis sufferers having to manage the potentially embarrassing situations attendant on their frequent diarrhea.

Notable in those all too realistic examples is the need to minimize or in some sense render a symptom invisible. This is different from keeping the disease secret. The symptom itself is sufficient to cause embarrassment, to destroy ongoing interaction, or even to make the person permanently stigmatized. The problem is illustrated in drastic form by a schoolgirl who always attempted to get herself to the clothing closet in time to hide her short epileptic seizures—a feat she was able to manage for some months. And Toynbee, the historian, when a schoolboy at a boarding school, managed for much longer to hide from his schoolmates his difficulties in passing urine:

> Generally speaking, it was never a case of making water when I wanted to, but always . . . of doing so when one could. I felt it necessary to keep my disability secret . . . since the worst thing that can happen to a boy at his preparatory school is to be in any way "different"; so I went when they did to the school latrines, though nothing happened there but the increase of my envy. . . . I used various strategems. One was to ask to be excused during class, when the latrines would be deserted. Another was to stay awake at night and use the pot under my bed when the dormitory's other occupants were asleep, or at least when it was dark.[3]

For interactional management, agents of various kinds can also be useful: wives who scout out the terrain at a public meeting to find the least obtrusive spot and then pass on the information to their husbands in wheelchairs or on crutches. Spouses can also save the day: some even have prearranged signals with their husbands or wives so that when a symptom starts appearing (such as a runny nose) he or she will be apprised of it. A more dramatic instance:

> A husband, at a party, noticed his wife's temporarily slurred speech—a sign of her tiredness and pain from cancer symptoms—and since they wished not to have their friends know about this domestic secret, he acted quickly to divert her neighbor's attention and soon afterward manufactured an excuse so that they could leave the party without awkwardness.

When visible symptoms cannot be disguised easily, misleading explanations of their presence or occurrence may be offered. Fainting, for instance, is explained away by someone "in the know" as a temporary weakness from flu or some other reasonable cause. When a symptom cannot really be much minimized, then a spouse may attempt to minimize it anyhow by preparing other persons for the distressing sight or sound of the husband's or wife's affliction. The sufferer himself may do this, as when a lady with cancer who had lost much weight warned friends over the phone that when they visited they would not find her looking like herself at all—"I've lost a tremendous amount of weight"—and each friend who visits is very likely, in turn, to warn other friends what to expect.

All such tactics, it can easily be seen, tend to involve a considerable degree of personal and/or family organization in order that they successfully be carried off. Of course, a cooperative, tactful audience is also helpful. When there is failure on either side, interaction is badly disrupted and can end in consequences like epileptic invididuals losing jobs because their convulsive fits frighten other employees, or persons ill from neurological disease withdrawing increasingly from daily interaction.

SYMPTOM CONTROL AND DISEASE CONTROL

A further issue associated with symptom control especially highlights the social rather than the purely medical aspects of that control. This issue involves the different relationships that symptom control has to disease control.

To block the downward course of the disease may contribute also to suppressing the symptoms, as when the chemotherapy that is used to check the spread of cancer is also useful in reducing the visible signs of cancer. Of course, sometimes symptom and disease control can be opposed to each other, such as when a physician chooses not to give medication immediately because this would suppress important diagnostic signs. Sometimes, however, there is not much connection between disease control and symptom control: suppressing pain helps the arthritic person live more comfortably but does not really affect his disease. The same is true of the comfort care given in hospitals to a dying patient during the last days of life: hospital staffs have abandoned their attempts to save his life and are concerned only with giving care that will both keep him reasonably comfortable and help him to die with a maximum of dignity—and, not so incidentally, make their own work lives easier and, if they are involved with him, minimize the impact of his loss on themselves.

It is often said that when symptom and disease control are opposed or independent, then the patient leans toward symptom control and the health personnel toward disease control. That can happen, but sometimes it is just the reverse. The real question is under which conditions will that first tendency appear, and under which conditions will the calculus be reversed or the parties actually be in complete agreement? The answers to that question are complex. We shall be content here with some pertinent commentary plus a few illustrations.

First, pertaining to complete "misunderstanding": an elderly lady who suffered from three diseases—including one that the physician considered potentially fatal (cardiac)—abandoned her digitalis because it tended to make her nauseous but continued taking pills for her two other illnesses. When, however, the patient is not afraid of his disease or even denies he has it (as with some patients with tuberculosis), then he is only concerned with the appearance and control of his symptoms, though usually his physician is much more focused on the disease. In diseases where symptom control is possible at least to some extent but disease control is not, then physician and patient naturally will concur on the priority of symptom control.

When people are reminded that their disease *can* be fatal, because of an occasional crisis, as are asthmatic or diabetic individuals, then they, as well as the health personnel, are likely to be very attentive to disease control, especially when daily problems of symptom control are minor. When a progressively deleterious disease is understood to be potentially fatal, then, like the health professionals, the sick person is likely to read the symptoms primarily as signs of his retrogression and is probably more interested in blocking, or at least slowing up, that retrogression than in mere symptom control. When, as in fatal cancer, there is no chance of doing this, then both he and the professionals can agree that symptom control takes priority—and not necessarily just for comfort but to maintain a more normal social existence while dying.

LEARNING ABOUT SYMPTOM CONTROL

To return again to symptom control (quite apart from associated questions pertaining to disease control), the really important point about it is that those afflicted have to learn, in detail, about the symptoms and their consequences. The sick person has to learn the pattern of his symptoms: when they appear, how long they last, whether he can prevent them, whether he can shorten their duration or minimize their intensity—and whether he is getting new ones. Nobody can entirely or accurately imagine, without that actual experience, what are the consequences for his bodily movements, his abilities, his work, his daily or weekly moods, and his social relationships.

That the body has the capacity for disturbing surprises is the lesson of every newly appearing disease and of new phases of old ones. This is brought out with sad vividness by interviews with the victims of multiple sclerosis and other neurological diseases; they are continuously surprised by their symptoms—their falling down suddenly, fainting, unexpected clumsiness, shakiness. As in some other illnesses, their symptoms often come and go, at least at first, a phenomenon that causes them still further surprise and that makes very difficult their assessing of "what's going on." Even when a person knows roughly what his trajectory will be, alas, his body can still provide some awesome surprises:

> Diana came in in a distraught state. She broke down crying. "What is happening
> to me," she repeated, "there is something terribly wrong here."[6]

Above all, the sick person must discover his limits, that is, how well and for how long he can carry on, temporarily or permanently, despite them. To carry on physically, even at reduced efficiency, means learning also to do many of the things discussed already, such as devising and redesigning. It means also the planning of activities. Having learned when symptoms peak during the day, one attempts to link up that physical pattern with the patterns of the working or sociable day. If a housewife with cardiac disease tires early, she will attempt to get her work done early. A colitis sufferer, described in a chapter in Part Two, working in a barber shop has struck a bargain with his co-workers; he cuts hair during his relatively symptom-free mornings and does tasks such as sweeping the floor during his worst hours. One kidney transplant patient negotiated with his employer to come to the job late and to stay working until late, because that fit his daily symptom pattern. When patterns are uncertain, then it is much harder to schedule given activities. People with sudden losses of energy may have to warn their friends that appointments can be called off (as do cancer patients in late stages of illness).

An alternative is to seize the minutes or hours when they do have energy and use them for all they are worth. Persons with cardiac disease, in the months after their myocardial infarctions, for instance, may have to learn to do this, usually only after bitter experience, unless forewarned by another cardiac patient. Such individuals usually have to learn, also, that they are not much "good at sex" during late evening hours; in fact, in one of the few good articles on that subject, a cardiologist has urged patients to have intercourse much earlier in the day.[4] As he remarks, the reticence of both patients and their physicians results in little communication between them on this worrisome but vital topic of sexual activity.

Having learned the symptom patterns, one still has choices as to how to handle them. A graphic illustration of this point:

> A sculptor had colitis. He found that going to the toilet and cleansing himself carefully was less important than the time and expense required to recast his sculptural molds. So, in his private studio, he often elected to defecate on himself and his premises rather than to interrupt his work.   *Reif*

For most symptoms, one really does have options—and, of course, different people choose different ones. Thus, some epileptic people choose not to go out at all, while others control the consequences of potential public seizures by always having protective agents with them when outside the house. Again, when one knows that sitting in soft chairs greatly increases the probability of back pains, one can decide to refuse the hostess' offer of "the best chair" or meekly submit to her invitation.

> One young man who developed ulcerative colitis chose to leave college and join a tolerant hippie commune, where he lived with his symptoms sans regimen. He did this after struggling for many months to control his symptoms through a regimen that took up almost all of his time.   *Reif*

Thus the options chosen, whether temporarily or permanently, reflect personal values. And as noted earlier, those values may include dying quickly or "now," rather than struggling to control symptoms finally defined as unbearable.

REFERENCES

1. Davis, Marcella: Living with multiple sclerosis, Springfield, Illinois, 1973, Charles C Thomas, Publisher.
2. Goffman, Erving: Stigma, Englewood Cliffs, New Jersey, 1963, Prentice-Hall, Inc., p. 91. Goffman is quoting from Orbach, p. 90.
3. Goffman, Erving: Stigma, Englewood Cliffs, New Jersey, 1963, Prentice-Hall, Inc., p. 89. Goffman is quoting from "N. O. Goe," in Toynbee, P., editor: Underdogs, London, 1961, Weidenfeld and Nicholson, p. 150.
4. Griffith, C.: Sexuality and the cardiac patient, Heart and Lung 2:70-73, 1973.
5. Hodges, E.: Episode: report on the accident inside my skull, New York, 1964, Atheneum Publishers, p. 109.
6. Lowenstein, Prince Leopold of: A time to love . . . a time to die, New York, 1971, Doubleday & Co., Inc.
7. Ritchie, Douglas: Stroke: a diary of recovery, London, 1960, Faber & Faber, Ltd., pp. 63-64, 186.

CHAPTER 4

REORDERING OF TIME

From what has been noted so far, it is apparent that the symptoms, regimens, and crises of various chronic diseases lead to temporal disruption. Therefore, this calls for, and indeed forces, changes in the daily management of time. Since we have already touched on the scheduling and timing problems attendant on the control of symptoms, those topics will not be discussed again. Two other types of temporal disruption and reordering are worth our notice here because they can constitute such difficult problems for patients and their families. In the solution of these problems, it is questionable how much aid the health personnel actually give or perhaps could give under current arrangements for medical and health care. Patients and families currently seem pretty much on their own in handling their temporal problems.

TOO MUCH TIME

One that is all too familiar is too much time. That problem may only be temporary, as with persons who are waiting out the postcrisis period. It can quite literally, however, be a permanent condition if either the person is so disabled by his symptoms that there is little in the way of activity that he can engage in, or if he is so discouraged by them or not inventive in finding substitute activities for ones now impossible or forbidden. Some people may try very hard to be inventive and still fail, as with the lady who taught handicrafts, but now that her hands tremble she finds many crafts hard to do. She tried to invent new ones that she could do and teach but could not imagine any.

Among the consequences of too much time are boredom, decreased social skills, family strains, negative impact on identity, and even physical deterioration. Some of the poignancy of "free-time blues" is expressed by one person who said: "It hit me so fast. I liked my work. I'm a worker! Now I have such an empty life. I can't go out. I can't work." Even those people ingenious enough—or with adequate physical or intellectual resources to fill up empty time with new kinds of interests—still may find that time passes very slowly.

TOO LITTLE TIME

Just as common, but perhaps more subtle in its effects, is not enough time. The person's time can be sopped up by symptom control and by regimens acting in the service of that control. Agents who assist, caretake, and control may also expend enormous amounts of time on their particular helping tasks.

> Asked what kinds of activities she had of her own, the mother of a child with cystic fibrosis answered that she had none, and although she keeps telling herself "maybe next week" there never seems to be enough time.   *Benoliel*

That particular parent's temporal deprivation apparently is shared with others whose children have cystic fibrosis, for according to one study:

> "They did feel deprived of time and energy to engage in leisure-time activities and in interpersonal relationships. Most important, they felt that there was a decrease in time and energy for self." Furthermore, the demands on their time meant a proportionate amount of time was taken away from being with the siblings of the sick child.[1]

Not to be totally engulfed, the agents may need to get other backstopping agents (babysitters, housecleaners, cooks) or call for a review of the family's division of labor (the burden of a sick mother should be shifted to another sister, or an elderly sick father should live for a while with another daughter).

Occasionally, the regimens require so much time or crises come so frequently (one sickle cell sufferer has been hospitalized dozens of times) that life simply gets organized around those events—there is not enough time for much of anything else. As a nursing student describes a kidney transplant sufferer:

> Her life really did revolve around the necessity of the routines of her medical management. There was little room for flexibility because of the knowledge that a crisis could be precipitated by carelessness. She felt that she had to fit in whatever living she could between doctors' appointments and the daily pill routine.

Even just handling one's symptoms or the consequences of having symptoms may take so much time that life is taken up mainly with handling them. This can be seen very strikingly in the chapter on emphyscma in Part Two; the amount of time spent in resting by emphysema sufferers while in the midst of activities or tasks—with time fragmented or stretched out—is enormous. The same phenomenon is evident in the chapter on colitis, but it is characteristically true of other diseases also. Thus a very bad dermatological condition caused one lady to spend hour after hour salving her skin, otherwise she would have suffered unbearably.

Unfortunately, the persons who suffer cannot just abandon their bodies, whereas it is quite possible for kinsmen and other assisting agents to abandon them out of desperation for what the temporal engulfment is doing to their own lives. Abandonment, here, may mean shifting the temporal (and other) burdens to a nursing home or other custodial institution. Abandonment or not, certainly some family strain is the consequence of too little time left over for one's own pursuits.

TEMPORAL JUGGLING

The basic temporal problems—too much time, too little time, scheduling, and timing—involve patients and their agents (assisting, controlling, protecting, caretaking, and so forth) in a delicately balanced game of temporal juggling. We say delicate and balanced because whenever there is a downward change in the symptomatology or a change in regimen, or virtually any change of personal or familial life style, then the temporal arrangements are likely to be affected. A kinsman may spend more time at various functions: helping with the housework or with regimen procedures, or acting as a regimen control agent, or assisting with symptom management, or even becoming a protective agent. Changes in agential function, necessitating that more time be spent, may come about as the disease progresses.

The strain of sustaining some of these temporal arrangements, as suggested here and in preceding pages, can be considerable. The strain can be measured imaginatively in a kind of mirrored opposite if one considers what happens during those periods termed "symptom-free." Life, including its temporal aspects, then returns relatively to normal. The same relief occurs sometimes for kinsmen, even during crises, when they are temporarily granted more normal schedules and more time by virtue of handing the sick relative over to hospital personnel. Kinsmen are granted that kind of temporary relief also when the sick one goes away for a visit or a vacation, or when they themselves can get away for even a short while.

> A mother of an asthmatic daughter is finally sending her away to a special school for asthmatic children, finding release that way from the burdens of caring for a patient who has been back and forth, from and to the hospital "100 times."
> *Benoliel*

Of course, it is not just time—or even events in time—that they are all juggling. In fact, they are juggling—the point bears repeating—potentially fragile patterns of temporal arrangements that can be disturbed by changes in symptoms, regimens, the disease itself, social and family relations, and sometimes lessened finances.

REFERENCE

1. Rosenstein, Beryl: Cystic fibrosis of the pancreas. In Dombro, R., editor: The chronically ill child and his family, Springfield, Illinois, 1970, Charles C Thomas, Publisher, p. 29; reviewing the actual study by Turk, J.: Impact of cystic fibrosis on family functioning, Pediatrics 34:67, 1964.

CHAPTER 5

MANAGING THE TRAJECTORY

In a book reporting research on dying in hospitals,[2] the term "dying trajectory" was used, meaning the course of death as defined by the participants to it. It may be useful to think analogously about chronic diseases, for most of their trajectories also are "downward" in some degree. Like the dying trajectories, the disease ones have characteristic shapes, since they may plunge straight down; move slowly but steadily downward; vacillate slowly, moving slightly up and down before diving downward radically; move slowly down at first, then hit a long plateau, then plunge abruptly, even to death; and so on. The shape of a trajectory is not a purely objective physiological characteristic, since the sick person must be perceived as ill, and then there will be appropriate expectations about the course of his illness. Each type of chronic illness (arthritis, diabetes) or subtype (different kinds of arthritis) may have some range of variation in trajectory, but each certainly tends to have a general pattern.

CERTAIN AND UNCERTAIN TRAJECTORIES

For some diseases, the trajectories are fairly predictable. Their phases can be anticipated, and even the relative rate at which the phases will change. For other diseases—like multiple sclerosis—both the phases and their rates are quite uncertain. Of course, for any given person who is ill, the sequential phases may be fairly predictable, but when they will appear and disappear can be most uncertain. This matter of certainty and uncertainty is of utmost importance because the efficiency of social arrangements is so closely linked with the predictability of the trajectories. Uncertain trajectories help to maximize personal and familial hardships.

If a given trajectory is relatively certain, then planning and preparation can be made in advance of each new downward phase; that is, provided people act rationally on that certainty. (They may have had imaginary rehearsals, sometimes quite accurate ones, by virtue of speaking to or seeing people "ahead" of them on the same disease trajectory.) They can move to easier physical terrain before their mobility decreases. They can, foreseeing early retirement, save for it; or foreseeing death, as did one cancer patient, prepare a wife for independence by sending her to a nursing school.

However, if the rate of deterioration is unexpectedly speedy, then the prepared arrangements will be that much out of alignment. Paradoxically, even when the rate of deterioration is slowed up, there can be difficulties, such as when expected caretaking or assisting agents die before the ill kinsman's really bad decline finally begins, or when funds have been saved for the expected bad days, but inflation or some other contingency drastically reduces those funds.

Even when there are reprieves or partial recovery trajectories—with uncertainty in rate of phasing or in "how far back" the recovery will go—then the reprieves or partial recoveries can cause considerable difficulty both in daily living and in the making of social arrangements. Sometimes the physician actually knows the extent of the expected recovery but does not convey it to the patient or, if conveyed, it is not completely understood by him or his family. Thus:

> A surgeon who does kidney transplants said that customarily when pressed for estimations of how long after the transplant life will become relatively normal, he answers "2 years," although he knows that both his estimates of when and how normal are *very* approximate. One patient who took the surgeon's answer literally and went back to work full-time after 2 years "ran into trouble."

That phrase refers to trouble with social arrangements, of course, as well as to medical difficulties.

The same general issue was addressed by Fred Davis in his *Passage Through Crisis*.[1] This researcher noted that for children stricken with polio two different perspectives develop in the posthospital period, "depending mainly on the rate and amount of functional improvement demonstrated by the child in the home setting." A child who makes significant strides in physical capabilities tends to generate in his family "an aura of achievement and a frequently unrealistic expectation of limitless improvements." By contrast, when he shows little or no improvement a:

> . . . moratorium psychology takes hold. The vague, overgeneral statement by doctors and others that improvement can occur within 18 months following onset of the disease is interpreted to mean that if improvement has not already taken place it might still do so all of a sudden and in one or two great bursts "before time runs out."[1]

We can easily imagine how difficult it is for both sets of families to make stable social arrangements, given their expectations of these kinds of illness trajectories.

One sees a poignant instance of this same phenomenon with people who are dying when there is a pattern of decline-reprieve-decline-reprieve-decline to death. Reprieves are certainly welcomed by kinsmen, provided they are genuine and the dying person is not too much of a burden, but they certainly render the previous social arrangements unstable and are likely to call for considerable and hasty rearrangement.

> Illnesses associated with reprieve patterns . . . hinder full preparation. Reprieves spark hope, so that the family is never completely prepared for the death: they think the next reprieve may be complete, not temporary. Thus, even when the doctor announces a time of death, usually a few days ahead of time, the family members may feel that the "miraculous" return to life they have watched before might happen again. As one uncle said, "It was hard to fully reconcile ourselves since we've seen her revive before and she could do it again." When a pattern like this is established, the family may refuse to give up all hope even if the doctor tells them they must, which may put the family through many "tortuous" episodes— after each, wishing the patient had died. Further, the short notice he is able to give them is usually not enough to allow the family members time to reconcile themselves and begin preparations.[2]

Even when complete recovery from an acute disease is assured but rate of recovery is somewhat uncertain—as, say, in mononucleosis—the patient's social arrangements are rendered relatively unstable compared to those possible if his trajectory were more predictable in rate.

DIFFERENTIAL DEFINITIONS OF A TRAJECTORY

Because trajectories, as defined here, are not merely reflections of physiological happenings but are linked with people's definitions of what is expected of a disease, it follows that the ill person may define his trajectory differently than may other people. He might not see eye to eye with his physician, for instance, because the physician does not wish him to know all there is about his future; perhaps because he does not really understand, or wish to understand, what his physician tells him; perhaps because temperamentally he is optimistic and so cannot really conceive the worst, or has a tendency toward pessimism and so draws too dark an imagined future. Some of the considerable shopping around among the available physicians is not simply in quest for more effective symptom control but a search for physicians who have alternative views of one's trajectory and so will try other means to alter it for the better. In the case of predicted fatal diseases, the shopping around is for a physician who will not give up.

> Linked with lingering and reprieve-pattern illnesses is the ever constant hope that medical researchers will find a cure in time: "They are working on it constantly." Some families travel from medical center to medical center and even make telephone calls to research centers all over the world to see how close "they" are to "the cure," adjusting their preparations accordingly.[2]

Whatever possible difference of definition exists between the ill person and his physician can be paralleled by similar differences between the ill person and his friends and relatives. They may not really understand what his future is, since they have not been fully told or have not had sufficient experiences with his disease to know about its course. Perhaps they overestimate his normality, but sometimes they are more pessimistic than he. They can even treat him as socially dead considerably before he is biologically dead.

At any rate, regardless of the disease trajectory's shape, the chronically ill attempt, at every phase, to place themselves somewhere on their trajectory. They seek cues that suggest whether they are moving into a new phase, carefully watching shifts of symptomatology. They may also wait anxiously for the next symptom to appear, debating whether it portends a new phase or whether its presence is only temporary. Sometimes the doctor cannot tell them with accuracy; sometimes he can, but then they may not accept his assessment.

Understandably, ill persons seek to impress some definition of their trajectory, and their current place on it, upon others. They may attempt to give their own true definition or give a false one, one they do not really believe. They do the latter, for instance, when the truth might lose them jobs or status or "face." Sometimes, the ill person has to work hard to convince some people that his condition is not so bad and will get no worse, if it is important to give them reassurance, because of their great anxiety or their overstating of his illness.

He may also run afoul of the problem of legitimizing his views of his trajectory, since some people will not believe he is really *that* sick. Husbands and wives sometimes have to convince their spouses who simply will not face up to the facts.

> One cardiac sufferer of our acquaintance wished to step down from an adminis-
> trative position but had a rather difficult time convincing his associates, not
> merely that he had just had a myocardial infarction and therefore was unwell, but
> that he was unlikely to be able, for 3 or 4 years, to carry heavy administrative
> burdens and had to resign immediately.

Apropos of difficulties in legitimizing: certain diseases can be very painful or discomforting but the people who suffer from them are at a great disadvantage in not having visible symptoms to legitimize their condition. Unless x-ray examinations or other diagnostic procedures back up their assertions, other people are likely to think of them as malingering or maybe somewhat sick, but not *that* sick—or even as pretty neurotic. Sufferers from neurological diseases are often thought of as having "psychological diseases" before an accurate diagnosis is made. People who complain of unbearable back pain—which is notoriously difficult to pin down diagnostically—and especially if they have been through two or three back operations—are quite often given short shrift by hospital personnel when they come in "once again." Faced with these patients' persistent claims to pain, the staff tends to assess them in a variety of negative ways: as "demanding," "clock watchers," "manipulators," "malingerers," or "crocks." The patient's attempts to convince the staff that he really does have "that much pain" frequently only reinforce and increase the staff's disbelief.[4]

Proper definitions of a trajectory by others can be a problem even when a person is clearly dying. While most of his friends may believe it, some will either not confront the issue (and treat him as if he were not dying), while others may act toward him as if he were already just about dead.

> A friend of a lady dying of cancer said sharply to another friend, who could not
> enter the sick person's house without a mournful and depressed demeanor, that

she should "snap out of it. Sheila's not dead yet, and wants to be treated like someone who's still all here."

COMING TO TERMS AND ITS MANAGEMENT

Whether dying or not, a sick person has to come to terms with his trajectory and is asking certain people who are significant to him to do the same. To others who may be equally significant, he may, as noted earlier, offer another definition. He does this because he wants them to consider him sicker than, or not as sick as, he believes himself to be. An instructive and realistic instance of this differential presentation of the sick self is that of a young woman, a graduate student, quite ill for a relatively long time from mononucleosis, an acute and completely recoverable disease. While still recovering, she presented herself as follows:

1. To people in general, she passes as not ill.
2. To her friends, she is "fine, but" since she hasn't come back all the way yet. The same is true for the faculty in a summer school where she is soon to teach, so they will not ply her with too much work too early.
3. To her parents, she says she's recovered, because she wishes to reassure them.
4. To her roommates, she still has "ill aspects," is "not all right yet," a presentation she nourishes since it saves her from sometimes exhausting housework; but then again, they can see or sense that she's not yet fully recovered.
5. With the physician, she emphasizes her recovery because she is bargaining for more activity than he wishes to permit.
6. With her boyfriends, she has perhaps the most difficulty, because they cannot deal realistically with her being ill. "You'll be better by tomorrow— or in a week." Because she sees them especially in the evening, when more tired, she finds herself drawing limits in activity—about how late she can stay up and so on. And they are disappointed. One boy hasn't been kissing her because of *his* ideas of possible contagion and she has not been able to convince him that this idea is wrong!

At every downward step in a trajectory—if it is the kind that does not simply remain on a plateau—the ill person must reassess where he is and therefore what social arrangements are necessary in order to effectively manage his symptoms, social relations, daily life, and preparations for his life in the foreseeable future. Of course, other people have to do the same for him, especially those in his immediate family. In a genuine sense, any chronically ill person who phases drastically down, or up for that matter, becomes a new person in the house. If he now loses his ability to walk or climb stairs, it is quite like having someone else there—someone who has to be given crutches or be put in a wheelchair, or who now presents a most awkward situation because no longer can he climb up to his bedroom and so he must sleep in a downstairs room.

The same person is likely to become a new person to himself, too, in the sense that his body is no longer what it was and so to some extent "I am no longer what I was." In reverse, it is very striking that when the ill get reprieves or have partial recoveries, they almost cannot think of their recently very sick selves (without energy, for instance) as themselves. Thus:

> One woman, dying of cancer, who had such a reprieve simply could not get over the Helen that was but who right now is not that person, although fully cognizant that she could become that Helen again, and rather soon. Yet, that recent energy-less self is not and was not "really" her.

And:

> A man with cardiac disease remarked, now that he is 2 years beyond his myocardial infarction, that it is only during occasional bad hours that he can vividly recapture his "very sick self" who found even talking on the telephone demanded more energy than he could command.

CONSEQUENCES FOR PERSONAL IDENTITY

It should be obvious that a person's view of his trajectory and the shifting social relations that may occur as it progresses can profoundly affect his sense of personal identity. That, of course, is not news! But what is worth underscoring is that the instability of social arrangements brought about by a developing disease in turn feeds into the sufferer's view of himself and his trajectory and into his previous social relationships. Thus, with the multiple sclerosis trajectory, the phases and their rate of change are so uncertain that all social arrangements are rendered exceedingly unstable—therefore, so are the sufferer's social relationships. His views of himself cannot remain unaltered; even if his sense of self does not become hopelessly unmoored and negative, his very efforts to maintain his social relationships relatively unimpaired and to build the new ones necessary to handle his new disabilities will contribute to a changed sense of identity. (The ingenious student with multiple sclerosis mentioned earlier certainly has not the same self that she had when her symptoms were still mild, and not the same self either as before she began gradually to lose some of her eyesight.)

It would be much too simplistic to assert that specific trajectories determine what happens to a sense of personal identity. Certainly, they do contribute and quite possibly in patterned ways. The identity responses to a severe heart attack presumably may be very varied, but belief that death can be only a moment away—and everyday—probably cannot but have a different impact on identity than trajectories expected to result in slow death, or in "leaving me a vegetable" or in "perfectly alive, but a hopeless cripple." Quite aside from dreadful last phases, certain illnesses can profoundly affect the identities of the sick person because the diseases, or their symptoms, are commonly regarded as stigmatizing. Leprosy and epilepsy are examples. People with such diseases are therefore likely either to have negative feelings about themselves or to develop psychological means for avoiding self-depreciation.

As for the various illnesses that are merely annoying or discomforting or somewhat intrusive into social relations, their identity impact is perhaps harder to predict. Such illnesses may not have any perceptible effect on self-conceptions. For instance, people who suffer from chronic sinusitis or mild bronchitis or diabetes may simply develop routines for handling symptoms and regimens, without deep involvement of their identities. As they grow older, however, they may discover unanticipated increase of symptoms and then may have to come to new—and "deeper"—terms with their illnesses.

REFERENCES

1. Davis, Fred: Passage through crisis, Indianapolis, 1963, The Bobbs-Merrill Co., Inc., p. 107.
2. Glaser, Barney, and Strauss, Anselm: Awareness of dying, Chicago, 1965, Aldine Publishing Co. pp. 170-171.
3. Glaser, Barney, and Strauss, Anselm: Time for dying, Chicago, 1968, Aldine Publishing Co.
4. Wiener, Carolyn: Pain assessment, pain legitimation and the conflict of staff-patient perspectives, Nursing Outlook, 1975.

CHAPTER 6

SOCIAL ISOLATION

Now and again in the foregoing pages, we have alluded to the loss of social contact, even extending to great social isolation, as a consequence of chronic disease and its management. It is entirely understandable that this should be so given the accompanying symptoms, crises, regimens, and often difficult phasing of trajectories. Social relationships are disrupted or falter and disintegrate under the impact of lessened energy, impairment of mobility or speech, hearing impairment, bodily disfigurement, time spent on regimens and symptom control, and efforts made to keep secret so much about the disease and its management. It is no wonder that chronic sufferers themselves begin to pull or feel out of activity and communication.

The process may proceed very far, so that social contacts are maintained only by the slenderest of threads and with very few people; or it may be far less drastic and not permanent. In any event, we ought to regard pulling away or finding oneself out of contact as a tendency accompanying many chronic illnesses, linked with their trajectories and a variety of associated social contingencies. For our purposes, it may be useful to dwell briefly on some differences between voluntary pulling out and involuntary moving out, as well as on tactics used by patients and others to combat the tendency toward social isolation.

THE SICK PERSON WITHDRAWS

As suggested already, loss of social contact is furthered by some of the symptoms and regimens themselves. Thus a loss of energy means correspondingly that much less energy to spend upon friends. So choices may have to be made about with whom to spend less time or to cut out altogether. These kinds of choices can become especially acute during the last phase of a very ill person's life, as with one cancer patient who:

> restricted visiting by friends to just a few with whom he could manage to sustain conversation—except during his three or four reprieves when he would feel the need for more varied contact and would reach out to a much wider circle of friends. Because he was dying, the smaller circle seemed not, on the whole, to feel rebuffed during the reprieves, as otherwise they might have since then they saw much less of him.

It is thus not difficult to trace some of the impact on social contact of varying symptoms, in accordance with their chief properties. A face disfigured with leprosy, as previously noted, along with the possibility of "being found out" leads many to stay in leprosy colonies; they prefer the social ease and normal relationships that are possible there. Diseases that are—or that the sufferer thinks are—stigmatizing are kept as secret as possible, and he "passes." But it is with some relief that he is able to talk about it with friends who may understand. Some may find friends (even spouses) among the fellow sufferers, especially during clinic visits or at special clubs or associations formed around the illness or disability (ileostomy, Alcoholics Anonymous). Some virtually make careers—sociability careers as well as work careers—doing voluntary work for those clubs or associations. People can also leave circles of friends whom they feel might now be unresponsive, frightened, or critical and move to more sympathetic social terrain. Here is an epileptic woman who has used, or perhaps slid into using, a warning tactic plus moving to a supportive terrain:

> I'm lucky, I still have friends. Most people who have epilepsy are put to the side.
> But I'm lucky that way. I tell them that I have epilepsy and that they shouldn't get
> scared if I fall out. I go to things at the church—it's the church people that are my
> friends. I just tell them and then it is okay. They just laugh about it and don't get
> upset.

When symptoms and regimens begin to take their toll of social contact, ill people may make very considered choices between that contact and their willingness to put up with symptoms and even with their progressively advancing disease. One cardiac male, for instance, simply refused to give up his weekly evening with the boys playing cards—replete with smoking, beer drinking, and late hours—despite his understanding that this could lead to further heart attacks. Compare this with another man with cardiac disease who avoided the coffee breaks at work because everyone smoked then, and also avoided many social functions for the same reasons. Consequently he believes that people probably think him unsociable since his illness, but he cannot figure out how to stop himself otherwise from smoking. Perhaps the extreme escape from—not minimization or prevention of—social isolation was exhibited by one lady with kidney disease who chose to go off dialysis (she had no possibility of getting a transplant), opting for a speedy death because she saw an endless time ahead, dependence on others, inability to hold down a job, increasing social isolation, and her life now lacking in purpose. The physicians even agreed with her decision—her right to "opt for an out."

OTHERS WITHDRAW

Features of social interaction (when combined with symptoms, regimens, or trajectories) can also lead to very subtle forms of lessened social contact and social isolation. Thus dying friends are avoided or even abandoned by those who cannot face the physically altered person or even simply the torture of visiting. A friend of mine who was losing weight because of cancer remarked bitterly that a colleague of his had ducked down the street to avoid meeting him. Even spouses who have known great intimacy together can draw apart because of features of an illness: the husband with cardiac disease who is afraid of the sex act, or who is simply afraid of dying and cannot tell his wife for fear of increasing *her* anxiety, but who feels slightly estranged from her because of his inability to tell her. One gets a sense that women with mastectomies feel somewhat isolated even from husbands because of the awkwardness that grows up, not only about the surgical mutilation but also about talking of potential death; and the women do not know how to get others to talk to them about their fears of dying from their cancer.[1] During the last phases of a disease trajectory, a virtually unbridgeable gap may open between previously intimate spouses. As one man has written: "This 'mystery of inaccessibility' to the quality of her experience and suffering was to me almost the greatest torment during the last weeks of her life. . . ."[2]

But quite aside from the question of death, interactional awkwardnesses appear that increase the potential for lessened contact and a sense of increased social isolation.

> One stroke patient has written that when colleagues came to visit him, during his recovery, he sensed their boredom with conversations which he could not sustain. "My wife, who was usually present, saved the conversation from dying—she was never at loss for a word."[3]

And:

> A cardiac patient hospitalized away from his home town at first received numerous cards and telephone calls, but then once his friends had reached across the distance, they chose to leave him alone, doubtless for a variety of reasons. He and his wife began to feel slightly abandoned, even though they recognized that if only one person telephoned daily, the news would be passed around among a dozen friends. The same cardiac patient later returned to part-time work, appreciating at first that his fellow executives left him relatively alone, knowing that he was far from recuperated—and yet, he felt considerably "out of things." This latter sense of isolation was difficult to combat; the former was partially countered with kinsmen who lived in the town where he was hospitalized, for they repeatedly emphasized that anyone who telephoned "surely is talking up a storm about you with everyone else."

Withdrawal from others can be furthered, however, by excessive demands and changed personality after a crisis or as disease progresses. The most complete form of this, of course, is the abandonment of sick people. Husbands or wives desert or separate, and adult children place their elderly parents in nursing homes. With some kinds of chronic diseases, especially stigmatic (leprosy) or terribly demanding (neurological or mental illness or advanced geriatric diseases), friends and relatives and even physicians advise the spouse or kinsmen quite literally to abandon the sick person: "It's time to put him (or her) in the hospital or nursing home." "Think of the children." "Think of yourself—it makes no sense." "It's better for him (or her), and you are only keeping him (or her) at home because of your own guilt." These are just some of the abandonment rationales that are offered or that the person offers himself. Of course, the sick person, aware of having become virtually an intolerable burden, may offer those rationales also—which does not necessarily lessen his own sense of estrangement. The spouse who does not choose to follow the advice of abandonment counselors runs the risk, in turn, of disrupting relationships between himself and them.

SUMMARY

Lessened social contact and considerable social isolation are among the more pernicious effects of chronic disease. However, as we have noted, lucky contingencies or hard work and some skill at making suitable arrangements can counter the tendency toward social isolation. Again, it is worth repeating a point made earlier about those social arrangements: they tend to be all the more unstable for disease trajectories that are downward. In short, the worse the disease (or the worse its phase), then the more probability—other things being equal—that the sick person will encounter and feel increased social isolation. "Other things being equal" includes, however, concerted attempts by kinsmen and friends and, sometimes, by professionals to decrease that isolation.

REFERENCES

1. Quint, Jeanne: The impact of mastectomy, American Journal of Nursing 63:88-92, 1963.
2. Lowenstein, Prince Leopold of: A time to love . . . a time to die, New York, 1971, Doubleday & Co., Inc.
3. Ritchie, Douglas: Stroke: a diary of recovery, London, 1960, Faber & Faber, Ltd., p. 37.

CHAPTER 7

A BASIC STRATEGY: NORMALIZING

The chief business of a chronically ill person is not just to stay alive or keep his symptoms under control, but to live as normally as possible despite his symptoms and his disease. How normal he can make his life (and that of his family) depends not only on the social arrangements he and they can make but on just how intrusive are his symptoms, his regimens, and the knowledge that others have of his disease and of its fatal potential. If none is very intrusive on interactional or social relations, then the tactics for keeping things normal need not be especially ingenious or elaborate. But when regimen, symptom, or knowledge of the disease turns out to be intrusive, then the sick person has to work very hard at creating some semblance of normal life for himself. So may his kinsmen, friends, and, sometimes, the attending health personnel. Furthermore, even when their normalization tactics are working well, various ups and downs of symptoms, new or additional regimens, and the hazards of the trajectory itself, combined with any changes of relevant social contingencies, all potentially threaten whatever arrangements have been established for keeping his life and his social relationships as normal as possible. Much in the foregoing pages bears on this uneasy equilibrium between what we may term the "abnormalization and normalization of life" (as does material in Part Two). In this section, therefore, the commentary will be confined to a relatively few points.

Many of the tactics discussed in the preceding pages can be read not only as measures for symptom control or regimen management, but as attempts to establish or maintain as normal an existence as possible: like people suffering from emphysema resting artfully at their puffing stations so that bystanders will not think they are drunk; or someone who has low energy coaching his friends to expect rapid and unexpected collapse during conversations—they are not to worry, but to "carry on as usual" talking while he listens with eyes closed, until he has regained sufficient energy. Apropos of energy, one inventive child with a cardiac impairment, according to his pediatrician:

> . . . used to be especially fond of playing cowboys and Indians. He was much in demand as an Indian because they were always getting shot and he could rest while he lay down and played "dead."[9]

But consider even the mild symptoms exhibited by asthmatic individuals with runny noses or arthritic persons with mild pains. The former may explain his rhinitis as "just a runny nose" and his watery eyes as caused by "a piece of dust or something in my eye." "They just accept what I say, they can't disagree with me." A man who has low back pain was asked if he did anything to prevent others from knowing about the pain:

> Yes, I do. I either consciously try to walk straighter and throw my shoulders back—or else I just ham it up and play the old man—like I say I had a hard night.
> *Wiener*

FATAL DISEASES AND THEIR INTRUSIVENESS

Perhaps a good place to start the discussion of normalization of intrusiveness is to note how difficult it is to keep relationships normal when people know that a disease soon will be fatal. We have touched on this several times earlier, but the general point is that even if the sick person can forget that he is dying, many other people find it extremely difficult to forget this dread fact, even momentarily. They do not realize that a dying person lives for 24 hours a day, 60 minutes an hour, and does not necessarily wish to interact solely as a dying person during every minute. This point is related to "identity spread," which is discussed later, but here we are only emphasizing the especially intrusive character of known fatality.

Particularly instructive in this regard are the experiences of parents with a child who is unaware that he has a disease that eventually will kill him (cystic fibrosis) or that he is actually dying (leukemia). In both instances, "closed awareness" ("don't let him know") or secrecy are the ruling principles of family life. Otherwise, one treats the child just as normally as is possible, within the limits of the necessary regimens and the possibility of fatal crises. Children with leukemia, however, present a much more difficult problem to parents who wish to keep things normal in the face of a much more imminent death. Futterman, Hoffman, and Sabshin have described the anguish of parents' private anticipatory grieving while they strive to maintain a front before the child himself.[3] For much of the time, the child actually may look quite normal and live quite a normal life—but the parents have to work very hard at *acting* normal, unless they can manage to keep the idea of impending death at the back (far back) of their minds. That is a very difficult thing to do. In contrast, parents of children with potentially distant fatalities need not work so hard to maintain an atmosphere of normality in their homes, except insofar as the child may rebel against aspects of a restrictive regimen which he feels makes *his* life abnormal.[9] If, however, there is some possibility of a quick, fatal crisis, then the parents may oscillate between maintaining a normal family atmosphere and yet anxiously keep an eye on the potential crisis.

INTRUSIVE SYMPTOMS

What about the intrusiveness of symptoms? Some, of course, are not even visible. Unless the sick person chooses to show or reveal them, they are little likely even to disturb anyone. Some symptoms are perfectly visible but are not accurately read by people who do not have eyes educated for those particular symptoms. For instance, signs of leprosy may be perfectly apparent to knowledgeable health personnel or to lepers but most frequently are misread (as arthritis, burns, and so forth) by people who, if they knew, otherwise would treat the leprous person quite differently.[4] Visible symptoms, then, are not simply a matter of physiological appearance but of learned perceptual capacities. Nevertheless, it is certainly true that, "other things being equal," symptoms like twisted hands, limps, pollution smells, and slurred speech are likely to be noticed and that certain symptoms are more likely to affect interaction adversely than are others.

Identity spread

So powerfully intrusive are some symptoms that chronically ill people often experience what may be termed "identity spread." That is, they undergo the experience reflected in the common complaint made by blind and physically handicapped men and women: people assume that they cannot act, work, or be like ordinary mortals. Blind and physically handicapped people are continually having to cope with people rushing up to help them do what they are quite capable of doing or being treated in other ways as only blind or only physically handicapped. The same is true for the chronically sick who happen to have visible symptoms. Nonsick persons, especially strangers, tend to overgeneralize the sick person's visible symptoms. These come to dominate the interaction unless the latter uses tactics to normalize the situation.

Normalizing tactics

In the section on symptom control, we have seen tactics similar to the following: one hides the intrusive symptom—covers it with clothes, puts the trembling hand under the table. If it cannot be hidden, then its impact is minimized by taking attention away from it—like the tactics of a dying woman who has lost a great deal of weight but who forces visitors virtually to ignore her condition by talking cheerfully and normally about their mutual interests. An epileptic patient quoted earlier chose church people as her friends, remarking that she had coached them so they would continue to talk during her seizures, and offer her a drink of water when she came out of it, but otherwise go on as usual.

Sick persons, then, use tactics to make or keep a symptom invisible or, if it is visible, to reduce it to a minor status. They work hard at keeping their poise. In short, they do their best to keep control of the interaction.

> A husband described his dying wife's control of her hospital situation: gets the nurse to adjust her correctly on a gurney, tells the nurse where to put the bowl in case she gets nauseous on the journey to the x-ray area, where to put her dark glasses which she needs now for protection against the light. "I heard later, how,

> racked with pain and frequently overcome by sickness, she had cooperated in the jests and never . . . lost her composure and dignity."[7]

Or again:

> Another patient noted that he doesn't wish to make his girl friend "rack her brains to find comforting words." He thinks sick people do that, because the closer people "are to you, the more they endeavor to appease you and assuage your fears with unconvincing words of solace. . . ."[5]

A sick person may even control the interactional situation by making others come to terms with the reality of his illness while yet not letting that reality dominate. Describing her experience with a young professional woman who has multiple sclerosis, an acquaintance remarked on how:

> She brings your focus smack down on her abnormality, underlining it . . . at . . . one and the same time addressing you in a manner commensurate with young professional women who are actively involved in interesting jobs and doing it well, and at the same time making you address yourself to the very aspect of her which places all other impressions suspect or in question.   *Davis*

Failure of tactics

Among the sick people who have the most difficulty in keeping control of interaction are those whose visible symptoms are, by and large, frightening or repelling to others. Their symptoms tend to "flood" the interaction, affecting it so much that its usual character is destroyed. Instead, awkwardness, embarrassment, and even cruel rejection prevail. Under such conditions, the sick person may elect to withdraw almost totally from ordinary interaction, as did one man who could not stand being out in public with his parkinsonian trembling. (An alternative to such isolation for a very few kinds of sick people is to live in the company of others just like oneself.) The more usual outcome of inability to control interaction, however, is that as much as possible one limits interaction to close family or to friends with whom one can feel maximally comfortable. These latter have learned to live with the visible symptoms without reacting too obviously, or at all, to them.

"PASSING" AND CONCEALING

When the sick person's symptoms are invisible or the fact of his disease is unknown to others, then he has the option of "passing"—that is, he can engage in normal interaction because nobody will define him as nonnormal. Of course, if there is some possibility that his symptoms can be rendered visible (as with Toynbee, quoted earlier, who concealed his urinary disability), then he must guard his secret carefully. Otherwise, one can see the consequences in such stories as that of a middle-aged man who described, still with some sense of shock, having fondled (20 years before) the breast of a seemingly unresponsive date who, alas, turned out to have had a mastectomy operation. After such operations, some women are very anxious about their first appearances in public and very concerned that they should appear as normal as possible.[10] The same is true of those who have had other disfiguring, if publicly invisible, operations. For instance, the author of a book on ileostomy notes and advises:

> The worst calamity the new patient can imagine is that the appliance will fall off. The second worry he has is that people will stare. One or two leaves of absence from the hospital for an hour or an afternoon are reassuring experiences which prepare them for the trip home.[6]

Two researchers have reported graphically on the problems of concealment frequently encountered by lepers in a society that fears their disease:

> Thus, at times, patients will go to considerable trouble to maintain their secret, disappearing from family and friends, elaborately disguising their whereabouts, remaining confined or hospitalized (colonized) indefinitely, restricting social contacts, and/or, less often now than in the past, assuming an alias. In the effort to conceal, individuals may also refuse to seek treatment where they suspect themselves of the disease or even know they have it.[4]

While the person who successfully "passes" in the world of the normal reaps considerable benefits, sometimes the psychological costs can be high. Those who conceal illnesses, such as various neurological ones, that they believe are discrediting or dishonoring have to carry the burden of anxiety that their concealment may be discovered. At the very least, that discovery may be embarrassing, but it also could be humiliating or destroy friendships or bring about unemployment.

The newly diagnosed leper who decides to "pass" needs to spend a certain amount of time and psychological effort at "working through" his feelings about posing publicly as something he is not—that is, a normal healthy person. With leprosy, which can be potentially communicable, there is an additional psychological cost to the concealment: the leper then faces such difficult decisions as to whether to marry and whether to have close contact with his children or his friends. It is no wonder, as noted before, that many prefer to remain in leper colonies, thus avoiding any "risky encounters with normals."[4] However, persons who suffer from the usual run of chronic disease do not have such available colonies. They must decide to either conceal their illness most of the time and from most people or to reveal it fairly openly.

It is worth underlining that there can be severe financial penalties for failure to conceal some chronic illnesses, quite aside from the social penalties. Thus cardiac patients who find they cannot conceal their illness also discover how difficult it is to get back their jobs or, indeed, to get decent new employment: potential employers do not think them sufficiently able for normal tasks. Worst yet, people who are diagnosed as having sickle cell disease need to be extraordinarily careful not to let insurance companies know of those diagnoses, else they will not obtain life insurance or may speedily lose whatever insurance they have.

Becoming chronically ill while on the job and having too intrusive a symptom or regimen, or just having the disease known about, can cost the job.

> Mr. James, who had a job at a department store, expressed concern because now he's about to go on center dialysis and his boss may think he's not capable of holding down the job. He said: "How can I tell people? My boss? What are the people I work with going to say? They'll treat me like I was blind or had a hearing aid or something. I want to go back like nothing ever happened, but they'll say 'He's crippled. He can't do it.'"
> *Suczek*

DISCREPANT ASSESSMENTS OF NORMALITY

The possibility of disagreement between the sick person and others about the extent of his illness is, in fact, a rather general problem faced by all the chronically ill. The parties can disagree in two ways. First, the sick person can believe he is more ill than they believe. Examples would be when he chooses more invalidism than his condition, to them, seems really to warrant. Actually, he may be wiser than his physicians, as for instance when his disease has not yet been accurately diagnosed, so that his complaining is still discounted or partly, but erroneously, attributed to psychological factors. The consequences of such discounting include not only further potential deterioration but even moral accusations leveled against the integrity of the "not really sick" person. He is said to be avoiding work or responsibility, to be not facing up to reality, and so on. Aside from general disagreement about how generally sick he might be, after each crisis or peak period of incapacitating symptoms the sick person may find himself rushed by others, including his helping agents, who either misjudge his return to a state of improved health or simply forget how sick he might still be. Especially is this so if he does not evince more obvious signs of still being sick. All chronically ill people who have partial recovery trajectories or oscillating better-and-worse periods necessarily run the hazard of others discounting their quite possibly slow recovery. ("Act sicker than you look or they will forget quickly how sick you were and still are" was the advice given to one cardiac patient who, after his attack, was about to return to his executive position.)

Probably with more frequency, however, the sick person believes his condition is more normal than others believe. His friends and relatives tell him: "Take it easy, don't rush things." His physician warns him that he will harm himself, even kill himself, if he does not act in accordance with the facts of his case.

> Two pediatricians report about children with rheumatic fever that: "Activity is a sign (to them) that they are like other children and will not die. Many times a child will go to extremes as soon as the . . . acute phase of his illness is past to prove that he is physically fit."[9]

It sometimes happens that the ill person has accurately assessed how he feels, but others are still thinking in terms of where he *had* been. According to the same pediatricians just cited:

> The difficulty in a large proportion of rheumatic fever cases is to convince the father and mother that their youngster is once again [after an acute phase] ready to lead a normal life. Overprotection can be as detrimental to the child's ultimate welfare as overactivity.[9]

Another instance:

> Mr. James had had a kidney transplant and eventually went back to work, where he found himself having to prove to his fellow workers that he was not handicapped—doing extra work to demonstrate his normality. *Suczek*

A rather subtle variant of differential definition of normality is that the ill person may know how very ill he is but wish others to regard him as less ill and to let him act accordingly. A poignant instance:

> A dying man was trying to live as normally as possible right down through his last days. He found himself rejecting those friends, however well intentioned, who regarded and acted toward him as "dying now" rather than as "living fully to the end."

DOWNWARD TRAJECTORIES AND NEW LEVELS OF NORMALITY

Since many chronic illnesses have characteristically downward trajectories—even if long plateaus intervene between downward changes—the sick person needs to come to terms with where he is now. Said another way, he is in trouble if he does not make arrangements appropriate to his current physical condition. If he continues to act and live as if that condition were only temporarily bad and will soon improve, then sooner or later his arrangements will prove inadequate.

The psychological acceptance of a new level of normality, when it does not necessitate radically new social arrangements, is illustrated by the squared-shoulder comment of a man with Parkinson's disease: "I can live with my symptoms"—implying that he could at least sustain most of his ordinary activities despite some body trembling and occasional dizziness caused by his drugs. It is precisely when the chronically ill cannot make the new kinds of necessary arrangements or cannot settle for the lower levels of functioning that are destroying valued life-styles that they opt out of life. When friends or relatives will not enter into new and more onerous arrangements, necessitated by lower levels of functioning, then they in turn opt out: by divorce, separation, or abandonment. Those who are ill from diseases like multiple sclerosis or other severe forms of neurological illness (or mental illness, for that matter) are likely to face this kind of abandonment by others. But the chronically ill themselves, as well as many of their spouses, kinsmen, and friends, are remarkably able to accommodate themselves to increasingly lower levels of normal interaction and style. They can accommodate themselves either because of immense closeness to each other or because they are grateful even for what little life and relationship remains. They strive manfully—and artfully—to keep things normal at whatever level that has come to mean.

Of course, their successful accommodation to lower levels of normality— including the worst—depends on the willingness and creativity of all engaged in what is truly a collective enterprise.

> The process is illustrated by what happened to one mother whose family accommodated by moving to a house without stairs, by her friends who shopped for her, by her husband accepting a house which is not as clean as previously, and his acceptance, too, of a wife who must now use a cane and cannot frequently travel or socialize outside her own home. Later, the symptoms became more incapacitating, and this woman's mother arrived, uninvited, and "took over." She managed the house, did the cooking, usurped command over the young children's discipline. All this resulted in the husband's withdrawal from household tasks (he could not tolerate his mother-in-law) and with a general break-up of the very delicate domestic arrangements made previous to the arrival of this intruding—if self-defined helping—agent. *Davis*

However, the process of coming to terms with lower levels of normality is eased by the fact that symptoms and trajectories may stabilize for long periods of time or not change for the worst at all. Then the persons so afflicted simply come to accept, on a long-term basis, whatever restrictions are placed on their lives. Like Franklin Roosevelt, with his polio-caused disability, they live perfectly normal (even supernormal!) lives in all respects except for whatever handicaps may derive from their symptoms or their medical regimens. To keep interaction normal, they need only develop the requisite skills to make others ignore the differences between each other in just that unimportant regard.

REFERENCES

1. Benoliel, Jeanne Quint: Becoming diabetic, Ph.D. thesis, School of Nursing, University of California, San Francisco, 1969.
2. Davis, Fred: Deviance disavowal, Soc. Prob. 9:120-132, 1961. Reprinted in Davis, Fred: Illness, interaction and the self, Belmont, California, 1972, Wadsworth Publishing Co., pp. 130-149.
3. Futterman, E., Hoffman, I., and Sabshin, M.: Parental anticipatory mourning, Journal of Thanatology 4:243-272, 1972.
4. Gussow, Z., and Tracy, G.: Strategies in the management of stigma, unpublished paper, 1965, Department of Psychiatry, Louisiana State University Medical Center.
5. Kesten, Yehuda: Diary of a heart patient, New York, 1968, McGraw-Hill Book Co., p. 196.
6. Lenneberg, E., and Rowbotham, J.: The ileostomy patient, Springfield, Illinois, 1970, Charles C Thomas Publisher, p. 114.
7. Lowenstein, Prince Leopold of: A time to love . . . a time to die, New York, 1971, Doubleday & Co., Inc.
8. Mayer, Marlene: Coping with chronic illness— four persons' views, unpublished paper, School of Nursing, University of California, San Francisco.
9. Merritt, D., and Davison, W.: Chronic diseases in children. In Wohl, Michael, editor: Long-term illness, Philadelphia, 1959, W. B. Saunders Co., pp. 625, 638.
10. Quint, Jeanne: The impact of mastectomy, American Journal of Nursing 63:88-92, 1963.

CHAPTER 8

THE FAMILY IN THE PICTURE

All through the foregoing pages, we have seen how the ill person's attempts to manage his medical crises, regimens, symptoms, disease, and social relations have been abetted—and sometimes hampered—by his kinsmen, especially those of his immediate family. While physicians and other health personnel are perfectly aware that family members are "in the picture" and can be useful or harmful in conjunction with their own professional efforts, nevertheless it takes a pediatrician to write something like this:

> . . . certain major concepts . . . can be guidelines in the construction of optimal care plans:
> 1. Family involvement in a child's care must begin when the care begins and be maintained throughout all levels of care.
> 2. Family-child dynamics must be evaluated, diagnosed, and treated appropriately along with the child's illness.
> 3. Continuity of such treatment must be maintained in the home environment parallel to the child's care and follow-up.
> 4. There needs to be unified professional leadership in such treatment, just as in the treatment of the child and from the same source.[2]

Understandably, pediatricians find that they cannot easily ignore the parents (although sometimes the siblings are forgotten), since these so obviously act as crucially important agents of treatment (and transportation!), and also since the sick child's progress or deterioration is so often tied up with the impact of his illness on the family itself. In a volume like *The Chronically Ill Child and His Family*, from which the quotation was taken, those kinds of consequences are noted or detailed with some frequency and emphasis. Thus, for cystic fibrosis:

> Maintaining this therapeutic regimen puts a tremendous burden on the resources of the family—in most instances a burden borne almost entirely by the mother.[2]

Also:

> There are many families where there are two or more affected in the family. The overwhelming burden inherent in caring for [more than one affected child] . . . needs little elaboration.[2]

For children with congenital heart conditions:

> Parents are tortured by guilt about prenatal cigarette smoking, x-ray therapy, tranquilizer use, even exercise.
>
> Many parents, often with adequate incomes, never go out together, as they fear leaving their baby with a sitter.
>
> Parent conflicts can erupt over handling of a fragile infant. . . . Many young fathers (and some mothers) have blurred their worry over the uncertain future [of the child] and its continuing expense with alcohol.[2]

For the nephrotic syndrome:

> Anxiety and guilt are apparent to some degree in almost all cases, especially in the parents. . . . Was it the cold remedy I gave him?. . . Did I neglect the early symptoms? Many parents . . . are seriously depressed and must be supported and encouraged. . . . Family conflicts may be created. Parents, especially the mother, may become overpermissive and overprotective toward the patient. This may exaggerate sibling rivalry.[2]

In short, the child's family is part and parcel of the medical situation.

The same can be said, of course, for adults who are chronically ill. Kinsmen need to act as various kinds of agents: protective, assisting, rescue, control, redesigning, "covering" in interaction, and the like. Sometimes they do those jobs magnificently; sometimes, for a variety of reasons, they refuse to do them. How they perform as agents may make all the difference in whether the sick person grows better or worse, or even whether he survives for very long.[1]

Another very general way of grasping the family's significance is to think about how the medical situation is affected by changes in the family's various areas of life. Sex and intimacy can be affected. Everyday mood and interpersonal relations can be affected. Visiting friends and engaging in other leisure time activities can be affected. Conflicts can be engendered by increased expenses stemming from unemployment and the medical treatment. Of course, as has been suggested, different illnesses may have different kinds of impact on such areas of family life, just as they probably will call for different kinds of helpful agents.

The message, then, is clear. Even from the standpoint of health personnel— let alone from the standpoint of the patient himself—chronic illness cannot be managed effectively without taking into account the ill person's relationships with his kinsmen—and, I might add, a very sensitive "taking into account." In short, if the reader will look again at the pediatric guidelines, quoted before, he will find that the guidelines could just as easily be applied to the care of adult patients. All that needs to be done is to strike the term "child" from each sentence and substitute "ill person." That is really very good advice, is it not?

REFERENCES

1. Calkins, Kathy: Shouldering a burden, Omega 3:23-36, 1972.
2. Debuskey, M., editor: The chronically ill child and his family, Springfield, Illinois, 1970, Charles C Thomas, Publisher, pp. 27, 40, 41, 63, 184-185.

PART TWO

SPECIFIC CHRONIC CONDITIONS
AND THEIR IMPLICATIONS

CHAPTER 9

THE BURDEN OF RHEUMATOID ARTHRITIS*

CAROLYN L. WIENER

RESOURCE REDUCTION AND UNCERTAINTY

Rheumatoid arthritis is a systemic disease affecting connective or supporting tissues. Its etiology is unknown, but the result is that the involved tissue becomes inflamed. When the disease attacks joint tissue, pain becomes the signal for patient and physician. In most cases, the onset is insidious, with ill defined aching and stiffness. In about one-fifth of the cases, severe multiple joint inflammation develops suddenly at onset.[4]

The victim of rheumatoid arthritis is faced with a reduction of personal resources—resources taken for granted by the healthy. More than one kind of resource can be profoundly affected. Mobility may be reduced because of the incapacitating effect of pain, and because weight-bearing joints are so deformed or acutely inflamed as to prevent the arthritic from wearing shoes and to make walking difficult or impossible. A reduction of skill may occur, attributable to increased pain, loss of dexterity, and loss of strength. Joints are not only swollen and painful, but have limited movement. A progressive disease, it can lead to dislocation of fingers and deformity of the hands. A weakening and then wasting of muscle may occur above and below the affected joint, causing a loss of strength. Pots become too heavy to lift, handbags too heavy to carry, doors too heavy to open. Finally, a reduction of energy can occur, caused by the metabolic effect of the disease (its attack on connective tissues) and also by the circuitous quality of pain (pain drains energy and fatigue produces more pain).

Rheumatoid arthritis patients learn, along with their diagnoses, that the

---

*This case is a modified version of a paper, The burden of rheumatic arthritis: tolerating the uncertainty, Social Science and Medicine, 1975. Most of the patients in study were chosen on a random basis from the files of the Arthritis Clinic of a major medical center and interviewed either in the clinic or in their homes; the rest were interviewed as in-patients in the orthopedic unit. Of the twenty-one patients seen, sixteen were women, five men. The ratio and closure figure were determined strictly by availability; however, as reported in the *Primer on the Rheumatic Diseases* published by the Arthritis Foundation, medical studies of rheumatic arthritis affirm that women are affected three times as frequently as men.

disease is not only incurable, but its specific manifestations are unpredictable. Often as not, they hear the physician say, "You're going to have to learn to live with it." The disease imposes a burden which many patients would assess to be a less "livable" condition than merely reduced resources, however, and that is its total absence of predictability. The disease does not often follow a strictly downhill course. Most cases are marked by flare-up and remission. Even in the most hopeful case, bad flare-ups may suddenly occur, just as the most severe case may suddenly and inexplicably become arrested. The disease has been referred to as a "rheumatic iceberg," in that the duration is lifelong even when so quiescent as to be no problem,[1] but quiescence and flare-up are themselves unpredictable.

The variability of progression severity and areas of involvement among these arthritics cannot be stressed enough.[1,2,5] For example, they may have reduced mobility but no impairment of skill, reduced energy but no interference with mobility, reduced energy one day and renewed energy the next day. Loss of skill will remain fairly constant if it is caused by deformity, but is variable if caused by swelling. The other resources (mobility and energy) can also fluctuate. Thus uncertainty pervades the life of arthritics: on any given day, he does not know beforehand about symptoms: 1) presence (if there will be *any* pain, swelling or stiffness); 2) place (area of bodily involvement); 3) quantity (degree of disabling intensity); 4) temporality (whether the onset will be gradual or sudden, as well as duration and frequency of flare-ups).

Pressing their claims upon the arthritic in consequence are two imperatives: the inner, or physiological world, monitored for pain and disability readings by the day, sometimes the hour; and the outer world of activity, of maintaining what is perceived as a normal existence. Like two runners in a nightmare race, these two imperatives gain one on each other, only to be overtaken again and again.

When the physiological world gains a lead, the arthritic finds that severe pain is more easily endured by withdrawing from interaction: "I go off by myself . . . to cry, or swear, or both." If these flare-up periods increase, both in duration and frequency, the uncertainty problem will be resolved by the certainty of more bad days than good. The activity world, to extend the metaphor, will have lost the race. The arthritic will have become an invalid and increasingly isolated. But the very uncertainty which makes the disease so intolerable also mitigates against acceptance of invalidism—there is always hope for another remission.

THE HOPE AND THE DREAD

All illnesses provoke theories of causation—circumstantial relationships as discerned by the patient—and rheumatoid arthritis is no exception. Part of his psychological toleration stems from his hope that a remission can be correlated with something he can control, such as diet. Belief in dietary causal linkage may be sustained for a long period, only to be upset by another flare-up.

Hope is primarily directed, however, toward control of symptoms. Uncertainty as to how long a given flare-up will last makes an arthritic vulnerable to folk remedies suggested by friends, kinsmen, other patients and by the arthritic's own reading of literature. Self-doctoring ranges from ingestion of celery juice or massive doses of vitamin E, to use of plastic bags filled with powdered sulphur and wrapped around the feet at night, or to a poultice of ginger root steeped in vodka and an alloy. The clinic provides a place where such ideas can be exchanged. In addition, there is a trial and error approach to the use of applied heat and change of climate, diet and appliances.

Even if relieved, arthritics are haunted again by uncertainty, for what they have attributed to a specific relief measure may indeed have been an independent spontaneous remission; but they continue to hope until proven wrong. When a measure is believed to be providing temporary relief, as acupuncture is presently doing for some, the hope becomes extended: "Maybe some week the two days relief I'm getting will become three." The reversal of the hope for remission (i.e. the hope that the arthritis will perform "on cue"), is of course less common. But that this hope can also be felt serves to emphasize the exasperating quality of the uncertainty. One patient reported she waited six weeks for an appointment with an acupuncturist, then was refused treatment because the disease was in remission and might be reactivated by the treatment. Even those whose deformities make their invalidism appear to others as irreversible, have so often experienced the oscillations of flare-up and remission that they continue to hope. One man, almost totally incapacitated by his disease, had driven miles to the clinic and waited there four hours for what turned out only to be a refill on his prescription. He explained his patience to the interviewer, "Maybe if you're around when they find something new, they'll try it on you." Similarly, a woman who evinced almost total withdrawal from social contact, still hoped to return to adult school "some day."

Countering such psychological tolerating is the fantasy of disease progression. An arthritic may hope for longer and longer remissions, but simultaneously be dreading the possible course of the disease—the next place it is going to hit. As one expressed it, "I think of my body like a used car, waiting for the next part to go." In a clinic they see others who are worse off and when they say, "I'm lucky it's not in my. . . ." the implication is clear. All this leaves them constantly on the alert. Pain, when it hits in a new place, makes their uncertainty intolerable. Knowing the possibilities is one thing, having them occur is another: the arthritic must wait to see if the pain persists and while waiting his uncertainty is heightened. He begins to worry that the new pain is not really arthritis but something even more serious, requiring professional diagnosis. He is inhibited by a selectivity when reporting symptoms: "If I tell the doctor about all my aches and pains, he won't be listening when it's really important."

The dread of a progressively worsened state brings with it a dread of dependency, expressed frequently as "I don't want to be a burden." Some fear dependency on kinsmen so much that they will live alone at tremendous sacrifice. To illustrate, one woman, now forty-four, recalled the early onset of her disease, telling of her move then to an apartment and her struggle to continue working:

> It was harrowing. When I got up in the morning my feet were so painful I couldn't stand on them. I would slide out of bed and with my elbow and rump get into the bathroom. I learned to turn the faucets with my elbows.

For her, the activity world pressed on, in spite of the increased pace of her physiological world, and in fact brought her through this early period into a long period of remission.

NORMALIZING IN THE FACE OF UNCERTAINTY
Covering-up

Arthritics develop a repertoire of strategies to assist in normalizing their lives; i.e., proceeding with the activity imperative *as if* normal. The principal strategy employed is that of "covering-up," concealing the disability and/or pain. Variations of the following quotes appear throughout interviews with them: "If anyone asks me how I am, I say fine," "When I walk I walk as normally as possible—if I walked like I felt like walking, I'd look like I should be in a wheelchair." Covering-up does not constitute a denial of the disease, in the psychological sense of the word. As described by M. Davis: ". . . it is the rejection by the patient of the handicap as if it were his total identity. In effect, it is the rejection of the social significance of the handicap and not rejection of the handicap per se."[3] Unsuccessful covering-up invites the risk of interrupted interaction via offers of help, or questions ("skiing accident?") or suggestions of home remedies ("Someone at work suggested I try alfalfa. I wanted to tell her I'm not a cow."). Interaction, thus interrupted, impedes the arthritic's ability to view himself as he would prefer to be viewed by others.

There are various conditions under which covering-up is impeded. An arthritic who is subject to sudden attacks, such as freezing of the back with resulting immobility, is a case in point. One woman who had such an attack while visiting her home town found that she could only walk at a creeping pace—some of the time only backwards:

> People on the street would ask if they could help. . .the embarrassment was worse than the pain. I thought they would all think I was crazy or drunk.

Visibility—use of a cane or crutches, wincing when arising from a chair or getting out of a car—is another impediment to covering-up. When the arthritic has the additional problem of deformity, the potential for covering-up is further reduced. Inability to cover-up leads to reactions such as evinced during an interview by a young woman who had struggled to remove coins from her wallet with badly deformed fingers. She said poignantly:

> I have just become aware of how uncomfortable people get around me. They don't want to be reminded of sickness; they are fearful for themselves, just as young people don't want to be around old people.

If covering-up is successful, a price may be paid, however, because this strategy can drain the person's already depleted energy. ("Do you know the stress you put your body to trying to walk straight so people won't see you can't walk?") Concomitantly, there is increased awareness of pain and stiffness once within the confines of the home. Patients report that after situations in which they "toughed it out," they give in to their fatigue and nervousness, dumping their irritability upon close family members.

Keeping-up

Armed with their strategy for covering-up, and lulled by their good days, arthritics struggle to keep the activity imperative ahead in the race, through efforts at "keeping-up"—keeping-up with what they perceive to be normal activities (preparing a holiday meal for the family, maintaining a job, participating in a family hike). They may carry through with an event successfully, then suffer increased pain and fatigue; but that risk is taken precisely because such payment is not at all inevitable. Keeping-up efforts may also continue—despite their seeming irrationality—in order to maintain self-images. To illustrate, one woman, who had a period of relief as the guest of her daughter, not being allowed to use her hands even to open a car door, suffered another painful onset the first day home when she cleaned her sink and bathtub, because "I hate dirt."

Another keeping-up problem occurs for those who have mastered the art of raising their thresholds of pain toleration. They may be slow to read the signs of body dysfunction as, for example, one patient who for a month walked around with a broken leg, thinking his pain was arthritic.

Some engage in excessive keeping-up—super-normalizing—to prove a capacity, or to deny incapacity, or to recapture a former identity. Hence pain-free and energetic days invite frenetic activity or catching-up. The result is often (but again uncertain) that time is really lost through increased pain or decreased energy the next day. Super-normalizing further ties in with the uncertainty of ascribing causes, as with a patient who knows her condition worsens during the summer, but is unsure about whether it is exacerbated by the weather or by her increased activities in her garden. Furthermore, some engage in super-normalizing as a device to distract themselves from pain. This too may bring increased pain, increased fatigue and sometimes fever.

Justifying inaction

Successful covering-up and keeping-up can even turn out to be a mixed blessing. Although his relationships generally remain normal, when arthritics cannot get by they then find it harder to justify inaction. Again this is related to the uncertainty of their physical condition—they cannot legitimize their current abnormality because sometimes they are normal; and other times, although hurting, they were covering-up or keeping-up. This difficulty increases when others have stakes in their remaining active, as with a young mother whose condition worsened when she tried to keep up in sports with her husband: "My husband really doesn't understand. He is very healthy and he thinks there is some magic formula that I'm not following—if I would just exercise, or have people over. . . ." Accusations may not always be so overt, but others' stakes are nevertheless troublesome, as with a tennis pro who found it necessary one day to cancel a lesson only to be observed out playing the next; he began to worry that his club members were suspecting him of malingering.

Paradoxically, arthritics who attempt to present a normal image to the world nevertheless are perplexed when not taken seriously by others. There is a longing for understanding, for a sensitivity by others, that goes beyond their justifying of inaction. An arthritic may be proud that "nobody knows" and yet wish that "somebody cared." The same person can boast of a mastery of covering-up ("If I went around looking like I feel, no one would want to be with me") and still say, "I don't think anyone has any idea how much pain I have." As expressed by another:

> Pain is essentially private. Sometimes you wish for someone to understand and be patient with your pain. To allow you to have it!! I do not mean sympathy or pity.

Pacing

Accompanying the use of the various normalization strategies is the really main one of "pacing"—identifying which activities one is able to do, how often, under what circumstances. Since these activities are what lead one to view oneself as normal, pacing is the arthritic's means of maintaining an uneasy equilibrium between the abnormalization and normalization of his life.

Arthritics know it takes them longer to complete daily tasks. For example, they allow extra time to get dressed, since putting on hose and tying shoe laces can be agonizingly painful. "I dress a little, lie down and cry a little, and dress a little more." They decide if they can work a three day week, or do housework for an hour; they know if they shop they may not be able to cook. Housework is not spontaneous, but planned around periods of respite. During remission, the arthritic may have resumed activities or assumed new ones, but then be forced by a flare-up to cancel some or all of these. Again the uncertainty factor operates: pacing is not a static decision, but necessarily fluctuates with the monitoring of the physiological imperative. Along with pacing decisions run all those problems mentioned earlier in relation to justifying inaction.

Decisions on activities (which ones, how often) are also affected by the time which is lost when resting between activities. Rest is prescribed, but not always honored, for symptom control; however, when pain and stiffness are bad, patients find they have no choice but to lie down. For some, rest becomes a ritualized part of the daily regimen—an anticipatory device for coping with pain and decreased energy. Time expended in rest results in a further cut-back of desired activities. It also may lead to a contingent existence. Since covering-up and keeping-up have become an integral part of the arthritic's mechanism for coping, many prefer to rest and then make a fresh assessment of the physiological imperative rather than suffer the embarrassment of cancelling plans.

RE-NORMALIZING: THE ADJUSTMENT TO REDUCED ACTIVITY

Re-normalizing, i.e. lowering expectations and developing a new set of norms for action, is directly related to the frequency and duration of flare-ups. This means, for example, settling for half a window being clean when an arm begins to hurt in the middle of the cleaning, or, as one put it, "Sometimes I cannot open a jar; I'll bang it on the sink, and finally say damn it, put it away and have something else."

Re-normalizing can have serious import if rheumatoid arthritis strikes early in life, as it did with one young woman who, instead of pushing to the limits of action, decided to re-define those limits. She recalled her decision:

> At one point I was struck with fear. If I got interested in a guy I'd have to be on the go and I knew I couldn't go out one night and then the next day. Maybe I set up enough blocks, so it didn't happen.

Increased frequency and duration of flare-ups will spiral re-normalization into lower and lower expectations. New coping mechanisms replace old mechanisms for tolerating uncertainty. For example, when constant use of a cane made covering-up impossible, one man adjusted with a substitute philosophy: "this cane opens many doors."

Eliciting help

Part of the step downward, of re-normalization, is the accepting of help. Arthritics in fact may have to elicit help—to be dressed, cooked or shopped for, helped in carrying out tasks at home and at work. If they live alone they may have to ask a neighbor for help with zippers and buttons. Once the need to ask extends beyond the immediate family, the act is weighed for importance. For example, one may consider asking a neighbor to unscrew the cork from a wine bottle but decide to forgo the wine; however, when pain and stiffness make public transportation a forbidding prospect, one will ask to be driven to the clinic.

Eliciting help threatens the arthritic's psychological tolerating for it reinforces his dread of dependency. Here is perhaps the most extreme illustration: one woman stood without moving for two hours, when her back froze while she was visiting a friend in a convalescent home. She would not ask for help but waited until she could walk home, one mincing step at a time. Throughout her interview she expressed her fear of "being a burden."

Hesitation in eliciting help also stems from the fear that others may not be responsive. Problems of justifying inaction surface again when others have stakes in action. One patient, who is supposed to wear braces on her hands at night and sometimes forgets to put them on, said: "It's too much of a strain to pull up the light comforter I use, let alone get out of bed and get the braces." Yet, no mention was made of eliciting help from her husband. This was the woman referred to earlier, who feels her healthy husband "really doesn't understand." Within their own families, arthritics have preferred tenders because of this matter of differential responsiveness. For example, one will only accept help from her son. His role was merged with his growing up. At onset of her disease thirteen years ago,

> My son was then five years old, and *he* had to take care of *me*. I'd sit on the side of the bed at night and he'd put my legs up, *he'd* tuck *me* in. Many times he had to dress me from top to bottom. My older daughter and sisters have tried to help me but I don't feel comfortable having them do for me.

Eliciting help decreases the arthritic's potential for covering-up and keeping-up. A case in point: the woman who took a leave of absence from work because she could no longer perform to her own satisfaction—she could not lift the heavy robes on her saleswoman job and could not stand having other workers do it for her since: "after all they're being paid the same thing as I". Deprived of her strategies for normalizing, she could no longer view herself as self-sufficient and capable as she wanted to be viewed by her co-workers. Lastly, awkward or embarrassing situations may occur when eliciting help and these only serve to highlight dependency. One man, for example, was forced to ask a stranger in a public toilet to zip his pants up; his fingers are closed to the palms of his hands, and he had left his trusty button-hook at home.

Since eliciting help is a tacit acknowledgment of the gain that the physiological imperative is making on the activity imperative, an additional strain on psychological tolerating stems from the identity problems which arthritics suffer when their eliciting of help results in a role reversal. Thus, a young mother told of her distress at being unable to pick up her baby. As he got older he learned how to clasp his legs around her. Now five years old, he must open milk cartons for her. She is anguished at her reduced capabilities as a mother: "My son wants to play games and I have to rest; I call him and he runs away, knowing I can't run after him." Male arthritics who have lost their dexterity must rely upon wives to carry heavy objects or open garage doors. Women frequently complained of their diminished role as homemaker using language like:

> I liked being a housewife and keeping the house immaculate. The house is my responsibility, and now my husband (sic children) have to do much of the work.

Role reversal may result in a permanent change in the household's division of labor. Helping out has now become a new job. Then, tolerating the uncertainty has lessened and dependency need no longer be a dread, for it is all too clearly a reality.

BALANCING THE OPTIONS

When tolerating the uncertainty, arthritics are ultimately engaged in the precarious balancing of options—options somewhat limited because of their already reduced resources of mobility, skill, strength and energy. Indeed, a balancing is involved in all of the pacing decisions (weighing the potential benefit of acupuncture against the climb up two flights of stairs "that will just about kill me," or the potential withdrawal from church activity against the loss of social interaction). The options are constantly presenting themselves, each to be met with an ad hoc response: whether to keep-up and suffer the increased pain and fatigue; whether to cover-up and risk inability to justify inaction when needed; whether to elicit help and risk loss of normalizing.

At the same time, another very worrisome balancing can be in operation. Arthritics may be put on strict drug regimens: the drugs hopefully provide control—to help the arthritic normalize. Patients with long histories of frequent flare-ups often undergo sequential trials of potent antirheumatic drugs, all of which can have adverse side effects.* Some have difficulty in recalling the sequence of these trials; frequently they were not told what was in their injections and did not ask. For them, the balancing was weighted in favor of relief at any cost: "When you're hurting like that you have to do something." Even after an accumulation of drugs, and faced with total hip replacement due to osteoporosis,† one arthritic attested she would have taken the drugs even if she had known the results: "I'm glad to have had those years of life."

There is a varying degree of knowledge among arthritics as to specificity of possible side effects. Usually the specific realization only follows an actual occurrence; even then, direct causation is not always fully comprehended. One patient who suffered from cataracts, which is acknowledged to be a side effect of cortico-steroid therapy, referred to her eye problems as "arthritis in the eyes." She was indeed also suffering from iritis, a recognized accompaniment of rheumatoid arthritis, but she did not appear to have made a connection between the cataracts and her eight year ingestion of cortico-steroids. Some when warned of the potency of their drug purposely do not ask for specifics: "If you know what to look for, your mind overpowers you." They are avoiding the potential strain of balancing.

Knowledge of the specific possible adverse effects of a drug heightens the psychological tolerating by placing an additional responsibility upon the arthritic. ("I cut down on the Butazolidin when I have a good week. Recently when I had a flare-up of neck pain I had to increase it again."; "I know when I take more than sixteen aspirin a day my ears start to ring.") Pain increases vulnerability—an arthritic may rationally resist starting on a drug with known side-effects, but when the pain becomes intolerable such resolution is tempered by the uncertainty of duration: "when the pain is this bad you feel like you'll never come out of it." The psychological burden is increased further by another uncertainty. What

*Soluble gold salts, antimalarial compounds, phenylbutazones, indomethacin, and adrenocortical steroids—generally, but not exclusively, in that order.
†A loss of bony substances producing brittleness and softness of bones, likely to be particularly severe during the course of cortico-steroid therapy.

"works" (i.e. keeps inflammation and pain controlled) for one day or one week, may not work the next.

Balancing decisions are therefore constantly being reassessed. One must decide what the options are, must decide between them by calculating consequences, must face the consequences whatever (uncertainty sometimes) they actually turn out to be; and one cannot rest easily or for long on previous definitions and decisions about options. Thus, about balancing there is at best only temporary certainty. This too, the arthritic must learn to live with.

REFERENCES

1. Bland, John H.: Arthritis: medical treatment and home care, New York, 1960, The Macmillan Co.
2. Bunim, Joseph, editor: Symposium on rheumatoid arthritis, Journal of Chronic Diseases 5(6):609-778, 1957.
3. Davis, Marcella Z.: Transition to a devalued status: the case of multiple sclerosis, unpublished doctoral dissertation, University of California, San Francisco, San Francisco Medical Center, June, 1970.
4. Primer on the rheumatic diseases, New York, 1964, The Arthritis Foundation.
5. Walike, Barbara, Marmor, Leonard, and Upshaw, Mary Jane: Rheumatoid arthritis, American Journal of Nursing 67(7):1420-1426, 1967.

ULCERATIVE COLITIS
strategies for managing life*

LAURA REIF

Ulcerative colitis characteristically manifests itself in the form of severe diarrhea. This means the sick person is faced with drastically different bowel patterns. Not only are his bowel movements more numerous than before, they are frequently spaced at very short intervals. Diarrhea often comes on suddenly and erratically, at any time of day or night. Voluntary control of defecation is extremely difficult to effect.

This situation persists for long periods of time, with the illness cycling unpredictably between exacerbations and remissions over the course of many years, not infrequently for a lifetime. Consequently, in both the immediate present and over the long haul, the individual confronts a disease whose impact on daily activities is observable, pervasive, and inescapable, and whose symptoms often defy prediction and control.

The cause of ulcerative colitis is not known. Medical treatment is aimed at slowing the progress of the disease and preventing physiological crises and death. It does not produce a "cure" in the sense that it removes or directly intervenes on the cause of the illness. Moreover, the regimen varies in its effectiveness; it is often quite limited in the extent to which it can ameliorate symptoms. The medical program, once embarked upon and if pursued as recommended, continues for long periods of time, and frequently continues over a lifetime.

For most, the disease stabilizes to the point where treatment can proceed largely on an outpatient basis. There may be acute episodes of illness which require hospitalization, but mainly the burden of treatment rests on the daily medical regimen which is implemented by the patient himself at home.

The specifics of the regimen include a somewhat variable combination of medications, special diet, corticosteroid retention enemas, and lengthy periods of

*From Ulcerative colitis: strategies for managing life, American Journal of Nursing 73:261-264, 1973, with acknowledgement to Anselm Strauss, Barney Glaser, Leonard Schatzman, and Marcella Davis for their comments, suggestions, and criticism on earlier drafts.

rest. The flexibility and intensity of the regimen may vary, but in general a strict adherence to it is decidedly constraining, for the regimen: 1) is time-consuming to learn and execute; 2) requires a moderate amount of skill to implement; 3) necessitates revising habits and routines to a significant extent; and 4) entails requirements which are often physically or psychologically stressful (i.e., prescribed drugs have dangerous or adverse physical effects; procedures may be uncomfortable, painful or repugnant to perform).

Both the symptoms and the medical regimen generate many problems of a technical and physical nature: the individual faces the task of coping with technically-difficult procedures, physical discomfort, pain, fatigue, various sorts of physiological disfunction, and even life-threatening episodes. However, many of the most important ramifications of this illness are personal and social in character. For much of the time these latter problems are the foremost concern of persons chronically ill with ulcerative colitis.

PROBLEMS OF POLLUTION AND TIME

Indeed, the two major concerns of the sick persons are perhaps: first, the personal and social consequences of the odor and excrement associated with their illness; and second, how the illness and its accompanying regimen restricted their use of time. Persons who have ulcerative colitis spend a great deal of time dealing with odor and excrement. They also face embarrassing social situations because of their diarrhea and its odors. Hence they face a pollution problem of substantial proportions. A large part of the problem stems directly from the symptoms: bowel movements are frequent, erratic, unpredictable, and often uncontrollable. Pollution problems are not only associated with symptoms, however; they also accompany various aspects of treatment. The sigmoidoscopic examinations, barium enemas, premonitoring preparations, and especially the daily retention enemas all have a great potential for creating problems with odor and excrement.

This illness also results in such demands on the person's time that usual activities and routines are often displaced or crowded out by illness-related concerns. Again, both symptoms and regimen contribute to this difficulty. The individual accords symptoms top priority attention: the personal and social costs of unchecked pollution are generally so high that few other concerns take precedence. Dealing with symptoms and executing the medical regimen take large amounts of time, even under the best of circumstances. In addition, diarrhea and regimen procedures often slow the pace of activity through interruption and interference with ongoing tasks, and thereby consume even more of the individual's time. Moreover, the unpredictable occurrence of symptoms and the specific timing required by regimen procedures cut across and into conventional schedules and hours. As a result, many of the sick person's normal routines and time-bound arrangements are disturbed or displaced by the temporal patterning demanded by activities related to illness.

In short, symptoms and regimen associated with ulcerative colitis complicate the management of time because they consume time, preempt time, and interfere with the structuring of time. The sick person faces constraints of considerable magnitude because time is a scarce commodity, time is unpredictable and unreliably available, and time is often available at irregular or unconventional hours. As a result, his time for usual activities is very limited, his schedules and planning are highly variable, and the hours he keeps are unconventional and often subject to last-minute changes.

This means that he can easily be out of pace with his associates, out of phase with the temporal requirements of his work situation, and either unavailable or unreliably available for various time-bound arrangements. Time problems manifest themselves most markedly when the sick person: 1) attempts to coordinate his activities and plans with others, 2) tries to meet the time requirements of a conventional job situation, or 3) attempts to follow through on tasks, personal commitments, or social occasions which have been scheduled in advance.

MANAGING THE CONSEQUENCES OF ILLNESS

Ordinarily the task of dealing with the above sorts of problems falls largely to the sick person and his lay associates. Medical personnel generally direct their major efforts toward preserving or restoring physical functioning, retarding the deleterious effects of disease, and preventing or postponing crises and death. While medical interventions are an essential ingredient in the overall management of the illness, additional sorts of actions need to be taken if the individual is to function effectively in the social and occupational realms. Mostly, it is the chronically ill person himself who insures the effective management of the overall situation.

Redesigning life style to deal with the consequences of illness

Because he is primarily concerned with the consequences that the illness has for his life style, the character of his interventions are markedly different from the typical medical approaches to the problem. Strategies largely consist of varying sorts of social and environmental manipulations and self-management tactics. That is, these ill people draw upon various resources—personal, social, environmental, financial, as well as medical—in order to work out new ways of handling his daily activities.

To be specific, they restructure the physical environment, utilize the help of others, or purchase special equipment and services in order to maintain themselves socially and occupationally. In addition, they develop ways of managing themselves physically, socially, and psychologically in order to circumvent or overcome their disabilities. For example, medications, dietary restrictions, and the kinds of special interactional ploys that will be described below are variously employed to sustain a normal appearance on the job or in social situations.

Selective utilization of the medical regimen

It is important to note that medical regimens are used quite selectively. That is, far from "buying" the treatment package outright, the sick person implements medical recommendations when they are effective for facilitating daily activities. In addition to judging the regimen in terms of its efficacy for improving the illness itself, he evaluates treatment procedures, medications, and other medical interventions according to their costs and benefits for enabling participation in valued activities and insuring attention to high-priority goals.

DEALING WITH POLLUTION PROBLEMS

Now let us turn to the problem of managing pollution. If the person who has ulcerative colitis is to carry on his daily activities, he must somehow deal with pollution. At least three approaches are tenable: 1) preventing diarrhea from occurring in the first place; 2) keeping odor and excrement from being noticed by others (protecting self and others from the disruptive effects of pollution); and 3) correcting damage or disruption resulting from pollution.

Preventive strategies

A number of different techniques are used to prevent diarrhea from occurring. The sick person can affect short-term control of symptoms by fasting, regulating his diet, timing when he eats, or in certain instances using drugs which provide temporary symptomatic relief. Over the long haul, he may obtain control of odor and excrement by restricting himself to certain foods, taking medicated enemas regularly, and utilizing a combination of drugs, varied to accommodate for changes in his condition.

While medical interventions figure prominently in such preventive approaches, the sick person's main criteria for employing a particular aspect of his regimen is that measure's efficacy for halting or delaying the appearance of odor and excrement. In an attempt to obtain this sort of result, some use opiates to the point of over-dosing themselves, restrict their diets to solid foods when they want to reduce liquid bowel movements, eat very little in order to cut down on the amount of excrement they produce, or avoid medicated enemas or diagnostic procedures which are seen as instigating pollution problems. That is to say, they do not always utilize the regimen as prescribed, nor necessarily employ it for the purposes intended by health personnel.

Protective strategies

Protective strategies allow the sick person to keep the odor and excrement accompanying his illness from impinging on others or becoming visible in social situations. Such strategies give him an alternative approach to pollution problems, enabling him to negotiate a large number of situations otherwise closed to him were he to rely solely on preventive measures. He lessens the disruptive effects of his illness by first, separating pollution-control activities in time and space from other pursuits, and second, concealing odor and excrement so that its presence cannot be detected by others.

The specific techniques for accomplishing this are many; the essence of the strategy, however, is to create conditions such that odor and excrement can be taken care of while away from other persons. Thus they carefully map out routes and places according to the accessibility of bathrooms. By restricting their movement in space to these "safe" routes, they are able to accomplish pollution control unobtrusively. When activities are not confined to familiar environs or previously-mapped territory, they employ tactics for casing new surroundings in terms of the location of toilets. In addition, some insure that they will not expose others to pollution by home-basing activities or avoiding travel and social encounters altogether when the risk of pollution is high.

Most ulcerative colitis patients probably also utilized some means for concealing and containing odor and excrement so that they will not be apparent or offensive to others. Frequent change of clothing, rubber pants, absorptive pads, and deodorants served this purpose. This strategy and the one noted above, while they do not prevent pollution from occurring, enable them to keep its adverse consequences—for both mobility and social interaction—within reasonable limits.

In connection with these strategies, some utilize the help of friends or associates to help them sustain ongoing interaction or activities despite frequent or abrupt exits from the social scene. These helpful agents are "in the know" about the illness and can serve as "front-men": they can be relied on to work in collusion with the sick person, to speak in his behalf to conceal his disability, to explain or justify his unconventional behavior or insure his "normal" identity. Protective strategies are often considerably more effective when coupled with the "fronting" or "covering" performed by the sick person's allies.

Corrective strategies

Another mode of pollution control is dealing with odor and excrement after they have occurred. Correcting the physical damage or social disruption occasioned by pollution is viewed by some individuals as actually less costly—in terms of time and effort—than interrupting an ongoing activity. On other occasions such an approach to pollution is unavoidable: preventive and protective measures are not always effective or timely. Moreover, some would rather tolerate the embarrassment of their problems being exposed to others than live in partial or total isolation. In any event, most have tactics for managing circumstances in which their problem becomes visible to others.

The person who regularly has recourse to this approach is adept at minimizing the deleterious effects of pollution on himself and others. Thus, he is a master of the art of quickly changing his clothes. He uses washable clothing, and easy-to-clean work areas, to help him repair disguises and environs with dispatch. He can deftly negotiate his way through an embarrassing social situation, helping others retain their composure while he keeps his own cool.

Many rely also on the services of "front-men" to supplement or assure the effectiveness of corrective tactics. In addition, post facto strategies are frequently buttressed by certain advance preparations. For instance, the individual who realizes that his control of pollution is tenuous may select or educate his audience beforehand, so that if an incident actually occurs it will not be entirely unexpected.

MANAGING TIME

Another way in which those who have ulcerative colitis insure their occupational and social functioning is by managing time effectively. This means conserving a reasonable amount of time for normal activity; and scheduling time, given unpredictable and highly variable circumstances.

Time-conserving tactics

Thus, they budget their time in an effort to utilize it more effectively. Time is portioned out in terms of priorities. Generally this takes the form of explicitly designating how activities rank with respect to each other along a temporal-priority scale; what minimum or maximum amounts of time should be spent on certain specific types of activity; and what activities can be left until last or cut out completely should time run out.

Another prevalent time-saving technique involves the routinization and streamlining of illness related activities. Routines incorporate certain time- and labor-saving devices which allowed individuals to handle symptoms and regimen as expeditiously as feasible. They simplify procedural techniques, modify room arrangements, improvise special equipment, and keep stocks of needed supplies in order to shorten the time spent on illness. On occasions, they economize further by omitting aspects of their regimen altogether, to conserve time for other activities.

In addition, they may make the most of available time by "piggy-backing" normal activity onto disease related activity. For example, many set up the bathroom as an auxiliary work area and set aside certain "lap work" which could be done while seated on the toilet. In other instances, they arranged necessary items so that they could read, dress, shave, or put on make up while occupied with handling symptoms. The time-consuming post-enema rest period was also used for various sorts of activity. One self-employed man routinely handled his billing and bookkeeping while "resting." They so organized themselves that they could fill available time on the spur of the moment by plugging in a stand-by activity. Others were able to increase the pace of work and so telescoped activities into shorter periods of time.

Strategies for scheduling time

People who have ulcerative colitis cannot rely on conventional patterns and routines to structure time; if they do, the interruptions which result from symptoms and regimen requirements are likely to upset many, if not most, of their plans. One way in which they schedule time is by monitoring their illness, then working out a temporal routing which tailors the timing of disease-related and social/occupational activities to one another. By observing how often bowel movements occur, how long they last, and the amount of leeway between warning and appearance of diarrhea, most sick persons can predict how much time is available, when it is most likely to be available, and what period of time can be spent in uninterrupted activity. They are then able to exploit the time which is most free from both symptoms and regimen requirements so as to do what they wish.

The success of this type of temporal routing, however, is contingent on the person's remaining flexible in his scheduling of time for normal pursuits; that is, normal activities must be fit to the constraints of illness. His chief strategy is to create conditions such that he can exercise greater control over the scheduling of work and social activities. If he can carry out his daily routines at his own pace and on his own time, he can generally avoid their being vitiated by illness-related activity. In an effort to do this, they work out temporal arrangements with employers, work associates, family members, and friends. Some had accomplished this to a remarkable extent. As a result, they were able to work at their jobs at irregular hours, work by contract or on a piece-rate basis and, in general, complete tasks at their own pace.

Most traded off tasks or work times with associates so they could put in time when it was convenient to do so. Many had elaborate back-up systems, so that if they were unable to follow through on a scheduled activity another person would substitute for them. On occasion, sick persons worked with other individuals in a "buddy" arrangement. The buddy (whether work-associate, friend, or family member) accommodated himself to the unconventional schedule and pace of the ill person and so insured coordination of activities.

In addition, those who have colitis often make special arrangements with close friends and family so they can deal flexibly with social occasions. These individuals are familiar with the sick person's unpredictable symptoms and can frequently make last-minute adjustments to accommodate for changes in his plans.

Clearly, the assistance of other persons is of great importance to the sick person, as he attempts to schedule time effectively. When he cannot insure coverage and coordination through the buddying or back-up activities of friends and associates, it is usually necessary for him to modify drastically if not completely curtail certain activities. Ultimately, this may involve switching jobs, quitting work, or cutting out social and recreational activities.

As an alternative, many who have chronic colitis attempt to modify the temporal dimensions of activities which are related to illness; that is, they attempt to regulate or delay when they deal with symptoms and regimen in an effort to work out a more conventional allocation of time. Generally this is most easily accomplished with those regimen requirements whose time and timing can usually be adjusted. Most individuals attempt to implement regimen procedures at times which did not conflict with their normal routines. Symptoms, of course, are more difficult to "time." However, the various pollution controlling strategies serve equally well as timing-strategies. That is, they allow the individual to stretch his time by staving-off symptoms or putting off the time that odor and excrement are dealt with. For example, by delaying a meal or wearing absorbent clothing, he can insure the time necessary to "make it" through a social occasion or to follow through on a commitment.

CONSEQUENCES OF EFFECTIVE MANAGEMENT

In the course of developing and employing various approaches to the problems generated by illness, the sick person substantially redesigns his life style. That is to say, over time he refines strategies until ultimately he works out a series of new routines which allow him to carry out most activities to his satisfaction. Activities, once conceived of as strategies for managing the problems posed by illness, come to be viewed by the individual as part of his usual style of living. At this point, he no longer thinks of himself as dealing with a situation which is out of the ordinary, nor sees himself as having to create special conditions in order to function effectively. He simply sees himself as getting along well. This is not to say that his life is as it would have been had illness not intervened, nor to assert that he leads a "normal" existence "like everyone else." It simply means that he is able to minimize many of the constraints of his symptoms and regimen, feeling that he can live with his chronic illness.

The foregoing remarks have a number of implications for health care personnel. They could help improve the situation of the chronically ill if they were to 1) give systematic attention to the social, personal, and occupational consequences of chronic illness, and 2) assist the sick person by facilitating the medical management of his chronic disease. This is not to say that they do not currently attend to these activities; they do. However, they could be more effective if they had systematic guidelines for both the social-psychological and medical counseling of the chronically ill.

CHAPTER 11

CHILDHOOD DIABETES

the commonplace in living becomes uncommon

JEANNE QUINT BENOLIEL*

Juvenile diabetes is a chronic metabolic disorder that is treatable but not curable, and the individual so diagnosed must receive daily injections of insulin for the remainder of his life in order to remain alive. Unlike the case of acute and serious illness where the physician retains control of medical management, the treatment of diabetes is characterized by a transfer of responsibility from the doctor to the patient and his family. Thus often quite abruptly, the parents of such children find themselves delegated an unexpected and somewhat awesome responsibility—that of becoming agents of diabetic treatment.[1] With little warning and limited time for preparation, these parents find that they must rearrange established patterns of existence to accommodate to the requirements imposed by the diabetic schedule and treatment demands. These requirements center around two aspects of life that many people take for granted as personal matters— *the management of time* and *the uses of food*.

MEDICAL CONTROL OF DIABETES

In principle, juvenile diabetes is treated by replacement of insulin that the body cannot make available on its own, in combination with dietary and living habits that keep the metabolic and physiologic processes of the organism as close to the normal as is possible. Because replacement by injection cannot provide the discriminating and on-demand release of insulin that occurs in the nondiabetic human being, the process of treatment must include an external and somewhat crude system for regulating the intake of food and patterning of physical activity so that the individual does not suffer the consequences of having too much insulin and too little available glucose, or, at the other extreme, too little insulin and too much glucose.

The key to medical control of diabetes lies with the management of time, and regularity of schedule is probably the single most important factor contributing to

*School of Nursing, University of Washington, Seattle, Washington. Research was done under financial support through Special Nurse Fellowship, 5F4-NU-10, 227-02, awarded by the Division of Nursing, U.S. Public Health Service.

effective medical treatment—and probably the most difficult to achieve. Side by side with regularity of routine is the balanced use of insulin, diet and exercise such that the individual suffers few and only mild insulin reactions (more properly, responses to hypoglycemia or low blood sugar) and does not develop ketoacidosis and the severe concomitants leading in the extreme to diabetic coma and death.[2] Without a reasonably regular pattern of food and insulin taken to cover the twenty-four hour day, the diabetic is likely to have episodes of low blood sugar and to exhibit such neurological signs and symptoms as confusion, irritability, convulsions, and loss of consciousness in the extreme.

Notwithstanding the fact that diabetes is a chronic metabolic disorder characterized as permanent and progressive, the availability of replacement therapy in the form of insulin provides the juvenile diabetic with the prospect of an open-ended future and the chance of living a reasonably "normal life."[3] The normalization of existence, however, depends on the diabetic's ability to follow a treatment plan that controls and prevents the acute and visible manifestations associated with disordered metabolism.[4] More than that, the maintenance of social order in the family requires a program of daily monitoring whereby the signs of these critical physiological events are recognized and forestalled before serious physical or social damage occurs.[5]

In the case of children with diabetes, the burden of normalization falls upon the parents who must adapt to the complex role requirements expected of agents of diabetic treatment. Concomitant with these new role activities, the parents must also modify already established patterns of family living to accommodate to the rigorous demands of the diabetic regimen.[6] It is the complex interrelationship of time control, food control, and daily monitoring to prevent physiological crises that cause the ordinary and usual events of daily living to assume uncommon proportions.

SOCIAL REARRANGEMENTS AND ROLE MODIFICATION

The delegation of diabetic management to the parents places them in a position of carrying two overlapping functions. They serve as *surrogates for the physician* in implementing a recommended regimen. They are *responsible for continued socializing of the diabetic child* to the norms, rules of conduct, and behaviors expected in the proper performance of the role of diabetic.[7] Thus not only are they to function as delegated agents of diabetic control, they must also act as agents of social control by providing positive sanctions for behavior that conforms to diabetic standards and by suppressing behavior that does not.[8] In both instances, parental choices and decisions are governed by the diabetic requirements for scheduled time and the disciplined uses of food.

TIME CONTROL

The influence of time in the daily living of the parents takes several forms. In the first place, they are the persons most responsible for fitting the new regimen into an ongoing schedule of activities that includes the other people in the family besides the diabetic child. One common difficulty rises from the timing requirements of insulin and food-ingestion and the pressured schedule that must be followed to avoid complications once the insulin has been taken. Under the best of circumstances in any American family, the process of getting children out of bed and off to school can be a demanding one. With the addition of diabetic procedures, the period before breakfast can become akin to a field of battle.

Each day begins by seeing that an early morning specimen of urine is tested for sugar prior to giving the injection of insulin. A useful test, however, requires a specimen that has recently been formed by the kidneys, and this means getting the child up to empty his bladder some thirty to sixty minutes in advance of the time set for getting the morning specimen.[9] Once the test is done and recorded, the parents then have to see that he has his shot of insulin and starts to eat breakfast within twenty to thirty minutes. Needless to say, the parents usually have many other things to accomplish during this period—such as getting ready for work, helping the other children get dressed, helping others get ready for school, fixing breakfast, and many other matters that are part of any family's preparation for the day.

Getting started in the morning is only one component of the temporal restrictions imposed by diabetes. The parents have to deal with the broader issue of rearranging their social activities, both at home and away from home, to coincide with the demands of the diabetic schedule. The burden falls mainly on the mothers, in great measure because the requirements of effective diabetic treatment impinge directly on the usual and ordinary activities of managing a household and supervising the activities of children. More than that, however, the new demands interfere directly with whatever free time the mothers may have for themselves.

FOOD CONTROL

One major change faced by the mothers concerns the matter of food control. Generally they carry responsibility for understanding the dietary requirements of diabetes and making some kind of match between the diet that is recommended and the family's usual pattern of eating. Regardless of whether they use a system of food exchanges or a system of weighing the food, the mothers of diabetic children face problems of figuring balanced meals, of restricting the child's intake of carbohydrate, and of insuring that he eats at proper intervals.[10]

Concerning the question of balanced meals, the mothers go through a period of being overwhelmed as they try to understand the whats and whys of food managememt. These reactions have two principal sources—lack of clarity about what they are doing, and the tensions of carrying a new form of responsibility for the child. As one mother stated, "I felt like I was holding a stick of dynamite."

The issue of feeding the child at regular intervals affects mainly two areas of family living—the dinner hour and the schedule of meals and other activity on the weekend. In families accustomed to an early dinner, little modification is needed in the arrangement of times for meals. Parents with a variable schedule of eating or irregular habits, however, may find themselves in the predicament of feeding the diabetic youngster alone and by himself or of shifting the regular dinner hour to an earlier time. In families where the children are still quite young, the weekends may pose no special problems in that the parents are accustomed to rising at an early hour. For other families, however, the practice of sleeping in is no longer a personal option for either the parent or the diabetic child in that effective control of the diabetes depends on a routinization of eating habits. In essence, Saturdays and Sundays become just like other days of the week and are no longer special occasions for eating and sleeping late.

A problem of singular difficulty is that of restricting the child's intake of carbohydrate, and the difficulty ensues because control of eating requires cooperation from the child. Although the mothers have some ability to control the child's eating practices at home, they cannot do so while he is at school or otherwise away from their surveillance.

Even at home, efforts to encourage the child to be disciplined in his eating habits run into many obstacles—primarily because eating is a human activity that serves many psychological and social functions.[11] For one thing, the child is expected to be an "outsider" in his food habits, and food for him becomes a "treatment" whereas others in the family are exempt from the requirement. For another, the restrictions on food and habits of eating cannot easily be enforced without sometimes a major overhaul in the family's usual way of using food. In a very real sense the mothers of diabetic children face the almost impossible task of teaching their children to be self-disciplined about food in a society that encourages self-indulgence.[12] It is not surprising that issues related to eating serve as disruptive forces in many of these families.

SCHEDULED TIME, CRISES, AND THE MONITORING FUNCTION

Although the parents are given general directions for implementing the diabetic regimen, it is generally through trial and error experience that they come to realize that having a diabetic child means being a clinical practitioner twenty-four hours a day. The true meaning of responsibility for diabetic treatment comes with the recognition that a routine of scheduled observation and daily monitoring for signs of untoward events is an essential feature of their new existence. In the course of assimilating these new roles, the parents sooner or later are reminded of how time-bound their lives have become.[13]

In thinking retrospectively about the early period of adjustment, the parents of diabetic children tend to describe themselves as feeling quite overwhelmed by the large amount of information they are expected to absorb concomitant with the tremendous sense of responsibility they feel. The mothers in particular describe themselves as feeling "tied down" or "penned in" and very concerned about the possibility of making mistakes that might do harm to the child.

The appearance of hypoglycemic reactions serves as the first warning for many parents that observation of the child cannot be viewed as a routine matter. When these reactions occur in severe form in the middle of the night or take place at school where the parents have to rely on other people for assistance, they are especially potent reminders that the monitoring function of the agent of diabetic treatment is a serious and never-ending responsibility. Not only must the parents become cognizant of the indicators that the diabetes is out of control, they must also become proficient in taking proper action in response to the crisis. More than that, they need to create a group of allies to assist in the monitoring function when the child is away from home.

With the passage of time, each set of parents becomes familiar with the warning cues and signs that are specific indicators for the particular child's response to diabetes as well as his usual pattern of behavior.[14] Here is a critical area where the commonplace becomes uncommon because the behaviors associated with the beginnings of hypoglycemia can also be triggered by other phenomena. For instance, irritability may be an early sign that the blood sugar is lowering, but it may also be due to a bad day at school or a fight among the siblings. The problem for the parent lies in making a determination that a diabetic crisis does in fact exist.[15] This lack of clarity about the origins of the behavior places the parent in a position of making clinical decisions in a situation heavily marked by ambiguity. It also places the child in a position of power for "using the hypoglycemic reaction" to get what he wants or to get back at the parent.

The ability to prevent and control episodes of low blood sugar in the child with juvenile-onset diabetes mellitus is not always easy to achieve. The child's need for and use of insulin is affected by many factors including his size, periods of growth spurt, variations in physical activity, presence or absence of infections, and states of emotional stress. The child's ability to understand and cooperate in eating the necessary foods is of vital importance, as is his ability to recognize the early signs of hypoglycemia and to eat properly while away from home. Thus even with the best of intentions and know-how, parents of these children cannot usually exert complete control over insulin reactions. The problem that they face is finding a mode of adaptation that provides some means for coping with these somewhat unpredictable contingencies.

Parents whose children are prone to have reactions at night, for instance, develop the habit of checking the child every time they hear a sound suggestive of restlessness. Through experience, these parents also learn that hypoglycemia associated with long-acting insulin does not usually produce the forewarning signals associated with reactions to regular insulin. Often these early morning reactions are not identified until the child is in convulsions or approaching that point. On such occasions, the youngster may be quite belligerent or unable to cooperate volitionally with the treatment procedure. Parents of such children tend to develop patterns of extreme watchfulness that can, in the extreme, lead to highly protective modes of socializing children to role-performance as a diabetic.[16]

MODIFICATION IN AND IMPACT ON PARENTAL ROLES

The re-establishment of social order within the family requires not only that the parents establish new roles as agents of diabetic treatment but also that they modify other established roles to accommodate to the changed conditions produced by the diabetes. Eventually the adult members of the household come to form a collaborative partnership with several distinct features. First, there is a division of labor concerning the particular roles to be performed—with usually one person carrying primary responsibility for being shot-giver, food-fixer, law-enforcer, record-keeper, or supervisor of the child's activities. The families also develop techniques that make it possible for the adults to substitute easily for each other in case of emergency, e.g. for the mother to become sick can in and of itself become an emergency. These devices are often in the form of written directions (notebooks or file cards) containing explicit information about menus, types of snacks to provide at bedtime, and proper steps to take in the treatment of low blood sugar or signs of beginning acidosis. Also, there is generally some kind of running account of the urine testing outcomes and insulin dosage that is used, and this record is used for continuing evaluation of the state of diabetic control—including reference to the physician.

Each set of adults also establishes rules of agreement governing other general matters: the child's time and activity away from home; the part to be played by siblings in treatment; the kind of talk to be allowed about diabetes at home; and the atmosphere governing the performance of the required tasks of treatment. Concerning the latter point, the meaning of the diabetes to the parents is a major determinant influencing whether the atmosphere relative to diabetic role-performance and/or conversation about the diabetes is one of openness or more on the secretive side.[17]

A critical requirement faced by parents has to do with the establishment and enforcement of rules of conduct for the diabetic child while he is away from home. In part, this means gaining cooperation from the child in matters of eating when he is at school or at parties with his friends. Because the danger periods for hypoglycemic reactions are usually those times just prior to meals, the parents also have to depend on and train other adults holding key positions to function as "treatment assistants." This reality means creating an army of well-informed allies who can recognize when a reaction is beginning and can see that the child takes some sugar or other fast-acting carbohydrate. In most cases, this requirement means having neighbors who know what to do. Each year the parents also go through the ritual of informing a new teacher about what to expect and how to behave in response.

As for rules of conduct governing the diabetic youngster's time, the children are generally expected to be home at specified times after school. Their activities in the evening are often limited to certain areas—usually within calling distance to the home. As for participation in events away from home, parental rules are based on a combination of factors that include the child's sex, age, ability to give his own injections of insulin, and parental styles of coping with the diabetes.[18] There is, however, a general tendency for parents to be cautious in allowing the young diabetic to be away from home overnight—even when he reaches the age of middle adolescence.

Accommodation to the demands of diabetes poses fewer difficulties for the family as a group when both parents are active participants as agents of diabetic treatment and they share a common perspective on the enforcement of diabetic rules of conduct. Conversely, accommodation to the change is tension-producing and difficult where parents differ in their approaches toward these roles or when a single parent must make the adaptation alone.

In any case, the commonplace happenings of living become unusual whenever the diabetic requirements overlap with the ordinary and usual functions of family living. Disruptions of social order tend to appear when the diabetes or the diabetic regimen interfere with already established roles, rules of conduct, parent-child relationships, and social activities both within and without the home.[19] Points of tension are those at which there is an impingement of the diabetes on one of three critical areas: the salient role-identities of one or both parents; mother-child relationships; and the spontaneous uses of time.

The personal and social significance of food and eating is clearly demonstrated in the variety of ways by which the diabetic regimen affects the lives of parents. For instance, one family of Scandinavian ancestry had to shift from a high carbohydrate and rich diet to rather plain and simple fare—a change that required the mother to give up a personal source of gratification, her baking. Spontaneous eating of candy and cookies is out of bounds for young diabetics, and food can become a critical issue within the family when other members choose deliberately to eat these forbidden foods. With eating on time a cardinal rule for the young diabetic, dining out is no longer a simple matter of accepting an invitation. Rather, special arrangements with the host and hostess in advance are usually necessary if the children are included in the invitation.

The impingement of diabetes on these ordinary events affects the parents in many of their other roles—at work, at home, and at play. In fact, they generally report a decrease in social activity away from home. Experiences that once were sources for pleasure are no longer readily available. For example, spontaneous activity—such as a sudden decision to take off on a trip—is no longer a personal prerogative for parents, nor is it an easy option when the total family is involved. Like their children, the parents find their lives are ruled by the clock.

THE FRAGILITY OF ARRANGEMENTS OVER TIME

The emergent and shifting nature of parental adaptation to having a child with diabetes is, then, its basic characteristic. The transition following discovery of diabetes requires that both parents and children make personal and social adjustments to accommodate to the demands of the diabetes, and these requirements can easily serve as sources for strain in family relationships. If tensions within the family are already high, the diabetes can serve as a focal point for the expression of unresolved conflicts and unmet expectations. The responsibilities required of parents as agents of treatment are in themselves sources of intense strain and psychological conflict. Furthermore, the process of "learning the trade" is fraught with uncertainty and unsettling experience. So, the potential for instability is always present in the changing symptomatology and social effects of the disease and treatment, and in the changing nature of parent-child relationships.

Even when parents have established workable patterns of functioning as agents of treatment, they are constantly facing new problems in diabetic management as the child grows older. Crucial periods occur whenever points of disjuncture take place—either in life-cycle of the young diabetic or in the family-life-cycle of changing parental responsbiilities and relationships. The movement into adolescence is one such period. It may be turbulent in the extreme if there are major changes in parent-to-parent relationships in addition to the experimental and testing behaviors of the young diabetic.

Clearly, the parent's adaptation to having a diabetic child is tentative at best and constantly shifting to meet new expectations and requirements. It is an adaptation that does not take place in a vacuum but in a social context of changing relationships. In a very real sense, the one characteristic that parents in such circumstances can claim to share is the common denominator of a high potential for instability due to a complex combination of changing circumstances.

REFERENCES

1. The transfer of responsibility implies a somewhat different relationship between doctor and patient/family than that conceptualized by Talcott Parsons and Renee Fox in "Illness, Therapy, and the Modern Urban American Family," *Journal of Social Issues,* 8 (1952), pp. 31-44. Several recent publications have brought into question the universality of the Parsonian model of the sick role, including Gene F. Kassebaum and Barbara O. Baumann, "Dimensions of the Sick Role in Chronic Illness," *Journal of Health and Human Behavior,* 6 (Spring, 1965), pp. 16-27; Eileen M. Callahan, et al., "The 'Sick Role' in Chronic Illness: Some Reactions," *Journal of Chronic Diseases,* 19 (August, 1966), pp. 883-87; and Gerald Gordon, *Role Theory and Illness: A Sociological Perspective* (New Haven: College and University Press, 1966).

2. Effective medical control of diabetes is geared toward the early recognition and treatment of these two physical states. In the case of hypoglycemia, the aim is to prevent damage to the brain and loss of effective cerebral functioning—the aftermath of low blood sugars for protracted periods of time. Concerning ketoacidosis, the goal is to delay the onset of the degenerative complications that sooner or later make their appearance in the person with diabetes.

3. As the acute manifestations of diabetes mellitus were brought under medical control, the lifespan of the young diabetic increased. So also did his chances for developing the chronic complications and sequelae long associated with the disease. According to Mimi M. Belmonte, "The Future of the Diabetic Child," *Canadian Medical Association Journal,* 88 (June 1, 1963), p. 1113, the future of the diabetic child is still clouded by these realities. His life expectancy is still two thirds of normal. After ten or twenty years, vascular complications in the eye and kidney begin to appear, even though good control has been followed. He is a likely candidate for the more tragic outcomes of blindness, uremia, neuropathy, and gangrene.

4. An explanation of the complex metabolic-physiologic process that occurs in diabetes mellitus has not been included in the article. One can be found in Alexander Marble and George F. Cahill, *The Chemistry and Chemotherapy of Diabetes Mellitus* (Springfield, Illinois: Charles C Thomas, 1962), pp. 13-72.

5. One of the most difficult aspects of diabetic control lies in the reality that human emotions have a direct effect on metabolic processes, and

situations that are threatening to the person have been found to produce rather sharp changes in the balance of body fluids, electrolytes, and metabolites. With the juvenile form of diabetes, reactions to life stress have been known to produce dangerous episodes of acute decompensation including severe dehydration and coma within a relatively short period of time, according to Lawrence E. Hinkle, "Long-Term Problems: Emotional Aspects," in Danowski, T. S. (ed.) *Diabetes Mellitus: Diagnosis and Treatment* (New York: American Diabetes Association, 1964), pp. 201-204.

6. Analysis of the detailed role requirements of the diabetic treatment agent has not been incorporated into this discussion. The vast amount of information and the complexity of what is expected of parents in the transfer of diabetic management to them can perhaps best be conveyed by listing the areas of instruction recommended for any hospital teaching program for diabetics. According to Edwin W. Gates, "Therapy: Teaching the Patient," in Danowski, *op.cit.*, pp. 103-107, instruction of diabetics should include these areas: (1) general information about diabetes, (2) diet—meal planning and exchange lists, (3) insulin-types and action, how to administer, timing action, storage, travel, prevention and treatment of reactions, syringes and needles, (4) exercise—its value, and relationship to food and insulin, (5) care of the feet, (6) marriage and parenthood, (7) urine testing—how and when to do and how to interpret, (8) control practices to minimize the complications of diabetes, and (9) general recommendations concerning medical care, identification measures, and other matters affecting the life of a person with diabetes mellitus.

7. In the sense that Peter L. Berger and Thomas Luckmann, *The Social Construction of Reality* (Garden City, New Jersey: Doubleday Anchor, 1966), pp. 129-47, use the terms, primary socialization of the child to his generalized notions of being a person and secondary socialization to the role-specific vocabulary and activity of a special sub-world (in this case, diabetes) are here performed by the same agents. Thus the matter of socializing the child to the meanings of being diabetic becomes complicated for the parents because it is intermingled with their efforts at primary socialization for membership in the society in general.

8. Lawrence D. Haber and Richard T. Smith, "Disability and Deviance: Normative Adaptations of Role Behavior," *American Sociological Review*, 36 (February, 1971), develop the notion that exceptional or "different" behavior may be defined as "normal" and acceptable through the formulation of new rules or norms that emerge out of reciprocal role obligations involving the disabled person and key persons in his role set.

9. For evaluating the state of diabetic control, the purpose of the urine test is to obtain an estimate of the spillage of sugar (or presence of acetone) *at that point in time*, and a test performed on urine that has accumulated through the night does not give information that is useful in making judgments about insulin dosage or the individual's general condition.

10. Diet by the exchange system is a plan whereby the individual selects his meals on the basis of specified allowances from the six basic lists of food substitutes, compiled in easy form in the pamphlet, *Meal Planning and Diabetes* (New York: American Diabetes Association and American Dietetic Association, 1950). One book used by those who prefer to calculate and weigh the diet in grams, Charles F. Church and Helen N. Church, *Food Values of Portions Commonly Used* (9th Edition; Philadelphia: Lippincott, 1963).

11. As Philip M. Wagner, "Food as Ritual," in Seymour M. Farber, Nancy L. Wilson, and Roger H. L. Wilson (eds.), *Food and Civilization* (Springfield, Illinois: Charles C Thomas, 1966), pp. 60-82, has noted, the utilitarian uses of food are of almost secondary importance to the ritualistic uses of food by the human species. Throughout the ages, eating has had many ritualistic meanings—hospitality, special tribal occasions (of which Thanksgiving is an example), and religious festivities. Thus food comes to mean many things to people other than sheer nourishment.

12. It has been well established that food preferences and eating habits are rooted in other customs, are learned early in life, and are not easy to change. However, in the United States the food industry through technology has caused changes in eating on a mass scale, and the phenomenon of haphazard and overindulgent eating has become commonplace—and not just in underprivileged homes. As Frederick J. Stare and Martha F. Trulson, "The Implantation of Preference," in Farber, et al., *op. cit.*, p. 234, have written: "The vending machine takes over the maternal role of providing the meal or the meals."

13. A clear contrast in the effects of time on human existence can be found in the uncertain, unpredictable, and disordered life styles observed in migrant workers living in labor camps; as Dorothy Melkin, "Unpredictability and Life Style in a Migrant Labor Camp," *Social Problems*, 17 (Spring, 1970), p. 480, has noted, the meaning of time to these people is "present oriented, irrational, and highly personal in contrast to the future oriented, rational, and impersonal character" of American time by middle-class standards.

14. As is so often true of signs and symptoms of illness, the behavioral manifestations of hypoglycemic reaction do not necessarily appear in a

form that resembles the textbook picture of what to expect. Rather they tend to appear as particularized patterns of response peculiar to the individual.

15. Barbara Louise Blackwell, "Upper Middle Class Adult Expectations About Entering the Sick Role for Physical and Psychiatric Dysfunctions," in *Journal of Health and Social Behavior,* 8 (June, 1967), pp. 83-95, notes that as the ambiguity of the symptoms of illness increase (that is, the signs have both social and psychiatric meanings), there are delays in help-seeking behavior among upper-middle class families—probably because the norms defining the sick role are not clear in the area of mental illness.

16. Four distinct styles of parental functioning as agents of diabetic treatment were identified in the original analysis of data. The four styles (protective, adaptive, manipulative, and abdicative) are differentiated on two bases—the emphasis given to supervision of the child's activity, and the delegation of responsibility to the child for specific tasks of treatment. A commentary on these four styles can be found in Jeanne C. Quint, "The Developing Diabetic Identity: A Study of Family Influence," Marjorie V. Batey, (ed.), *Communicating Nursing Research: Methodological Issues in Research—Volume 3* (Boulder, Colorado: Western Interstate Commission on Higher Education, 1970), pp. 14-32.

17. In two of the families, the reactions of the mothers had strong elements of shame tied to the diabetes, and they "felt sorry" for their part in bringing the child into the world. Both families were Irish Catholic, and each had a family history of diabetes. The child in each case was a girl just at puberty when the diabetes was discovered, and the *theme of shame* fostered a climate of secrecy that, in turn, was reflected in a serious disruption of social order in the family. In discussing differences between shame and guilt, Helen Merrell Lynd, *On Shame and the Search for Identity* (New York: Science Editions, 1961), p. 22, offers these definitions: "A sense of guilt arises from a feeling of wrongdoing, and a sense of shame from a feeling of inferiority." On p. 190 she also notes that the socialization of American children has placed a heavy emphasis on "right and wrong" that appears to be especially strong in families that combine a strong religious background with limited economic resources.

18. Protective parents tend to maintain a tight control over the young diabetic's time away from home whereas adaptive parents are found to use sex-graded and age-graded criteria for making such judgments. The abdicative parent is one who functions essentially as a nonparticipant, except when the diabetes interferes with his own activity. The manipulative parent demonstrates a variable and often contradictory concern over control of the child's time and activity.

19. A second type of disruption of social order comes about through the appearance of interfering roles that function as sources of tension in the patterning of social relationships within the family. The diabetes can provide a locus for disruption in four areas: the injection of insulin; the uses of food; compliance and noncompliance with medical treatments; and unwanted conversation about the diabetes.

CHAPTER 12

GETTING AROUND WITH EMPHYSEMA*

SHIZUKO FAGERHAUGH

SALIENCY

... Emphysema is a severe respiratory disease with irreversible deterioration of the lungs.

... The resulting paucity of oxygen intake means that there is a considerable, even major, lessening of available bodily energy. Any movement or exertion—even talking, crying, or laughing—uses oxygen and can bring about respiratory distress.

... The prescribed long-term regimen aims at preventing further deterioration and easing the breathing. The regimen may involve drugs, inhalation machinery, and spending time at breathing exercises and learning breath control; and may require daily, weekly, or monthly visits to a hospital or clinic.

Possibly the main problem of people who suffer from emphysema is the management of scarce energy. They may be able to increase their energy through a proper regimen. Primarily, however, they must allocate their energy to those activities which they must do or wish most to do. Hence two key issues for them are symptom control (energy loss) and the balancing of regimen versus other considerations. To those problems, we shall add, in the pages that follow, the matter of a worsening trajectory, and the impact of advanced age and of being poor. (The study on which this case is based was of quite poor people and mostly without supporting kinsmen. The choice of this population was deliberate, since their condition reduced their available resources for coping with energy losses.)

BASIC MOBILITY AND SOCIABILITY RESOURCES

Time, energy, and money are basic resources which all people draw upon for physical mobility and sociability. We have varying amounts of these basic resources (henceforth called BMRs) which can be juggled and balanced to allow physical mobility and sociability. In general, a generous supply of health and wealth permits much of both. In situations of decreased energy supply, due to

*Slightly modified version of a paper published in Nursing Outlook 73:94-99, 1973.

illness or old age, a generous supply of money can purchase other people's BMRs. Thereby one's own time and energy can be saved. A short supply of both energy and money, but a reliable and accessible supply from friends and family, can balance the decreased BMRs. How a person juggles and balances his BMRs depends not only upon his own supply of BMRs and the availability and purchasability of other people's BMRs, but also, as we shall see, upon his life style and life situation.

Translating the calculus of BMRs of the majority of the patients interviewed, they had a meager supply of energy because of old age and advanced emphysema. (In several instances their energy supply was further decreased because of other chronic conditions such as heart disease and arthritis.) Their money supply was also scarce since savings were depleted because of extended illness: their advanced disease condition did not allow gainful employment, and the welfare aid was far from generous. Because of being widowed or divorced for many years, or never married, other people's BMRs often were not reliable or available. They did have a large supply of time because they did not work and had no large network of close family ties and friends who could take up their time. In short, their BMR status and life situation tended to maximize their mobility and sociability problems.

OXYGEN SHORTAGE: GAUGING AND MISGAUGING

The mobility problem of the emphysema victim is primarily one of inability to get enough oxygen to produce energy. A certain amount of oxygen is necessary to maintain the body at rest; for physical activity a (lung) oxygen reserve volume is required. Depending upon the activity, more or less oxygen is necessary. In advanced emphysema, because of pathological changes,[1] there is very limited oxygen reserve, and maintaining the limited reserve is difficult. These patients become "short of breath" with minimal physical activity, and compared to "normal lungers" require longer and more frequent periods to "recoup"[2] their diminished oxygen reserve.

Because of the limited oxygen reserve and the difficulty in maintaining the limited reserve they must gauge the oxygen requirement for various activities with their "recoupable" supply. Correct gauging is vital because misgauging can result in dire consequences; extreme physical distress—a sense of suffocation—a chance of losing consciousness, and of course great fatigue. In fact, many expressed a sense of panic in misgauged mobility situations.

When normal people engage in activities, there is a fluidity and simultaneity about their actions. When completing an activity where walking, talking, lifting, or whatever is involved, each specific act smoothly blends into an easy flow. Also, when normals over-exert themselves they can pant a few times and continue with their action—no worse for the wear. Normal lungers can also carry out several activities simultaneously, like walking and talking. That fluidity and simultaneity of activity is not possible for advanced emphysema patients. The latter deliberately chop up the fluidity into smaller or smaller "recoupable" units depending upon their disease status. Also, their activities tend to get ordered sequentially rather than simultaneously in order to conserve energy.

Adequate lung reserve is necessary not only for physical mobility, but for such vocalizations as talking, laughing, singing, or yelling. Thus, when being mobile, someone with severe emphysema must consider when and where he will expend his meager air supply for sociability as over against other uses. Such expenditures of air must be calculated. Because of advanced stages of emphysema, extended talking, laughing, or crying can trigger off paroxysms of coughing as well as respiratory distress. Hence, some patients' social interactions tend to decrease. In fact, interviewing these people can be rather taxing for an interviewer since their typical conversational pattern is to talk a bit, pant for air, talk a bit and pant for air. Some remarked that they decreased interactions with others, sensing their discomfiture. Moreover, social situations which are anxiety provoking tend to bring on attacks of "shortness of breath." A characteristic of emphysema is that anxiety triggers dyspnea which brings on more anxiety, developing into a vicious cycle.[3] Over the long haul, with progressive lung deterioration, these people tend to isolate themselves as a defense against anxiety-provoking social involvements.[4]

INTERRELATIONSHIP OF BMRs TO LIFE STYLE AND MOBILITY NEEDS

Judgements concerning what to be mobile about are influenced by available basic mobility resources. Also, one's life style and life conditions will determine how and where the BMRs are utilized for physical and social mobilization. The interaction of the person's BMRs, life style and life conditions will shape his mobility priorities. Thus, he may simply delete or partially restrict aspects of his life style and mobility needs because of diminishing BMRs. He may compromise, making up for inadequacies in some areas of his life situation to provide for other higher priority needs.

For example, he must have priorities regarding features of his residential site and its territorial topography. The features of both include 1) terrain of resident location—whether flat or hilly, and terrain of residence itself—first floor, elevator or no elevator, etc.; 2) propinquity of and terrain to and from public transportation; 3) propinquity of and terrain to and from such essential places as grocery store, cafe, laundromat, and bank; and 4) propinquity of mobility assistants (family members and friends).

A patient with money can afford taxis and have groceries delivered. Someone with reliable friends and family with an automobile is not as concerned with topography or residence location or the accessibility of public transportation as patients without much money. Patients with limited money are often unable to afford a costly oxygen-saving residence. Moreover, because of lack of energy they are frequently unable to engage in extended residence hunting, and consequently settle for whatever halfway meets their oxygen-saving specifications. They must tolerate some bad residential and territorial features in exchange for other features judged as more essential in their life style. Here are a few examples.

Mr. B., a widower, always lived in an apartment; therefore he preferred living in an apartment. Being unable to afford an apartment with an elevator he settled for a second floor apartment within his financial means. It was located in a terrain which, although slightly inclined, was manageable within his oxygen reserve limit. This apartment was close to a grocery store. He liked to cook and stretched his money by doing his own cooking. Hence, accessibility to the grocery store was very important. His social interactions were limited primarily to the apartment tenants and the manager, all acting as his mobility assistants since they helped by picking up a quart of milk while doing their own errands. A particularly important fellow tenant was a man who had a car; he was useful for especially difficult situations such as getting to the clinic. Getting there by public transportation involved considerable time and energy and required several bus transfers. However, he was careful not to abuse the help of his friend, limiting his request only to those which seemed legitimate and reasonable. Once he was placed on inhalation therapy, which necessitated daily trips to the clinic. Feeling unjustified then in requesting daily assistance from his friend, he managed the clinic visits by public transportation. After a week of treatment he stopped therapy because the time and effort of getting to and from the clinic left him too exhausted to do other necessary tasks—such as cooking, keeping up the apartment, and doing his laundry.

In contrast, a bachelor with a network of casual acquaintances in his neighborhood, who met regularly at the neighborhood social club-like bar, chose both his residential features and how to expend his oxygen quite differently. With his deteriorating respiratory condition and the depletion of his money, he progressed to increasingly deteriorated residences within the same neighborhood where he had long lived; for instance, from a nice apartment to a single room on the second floor of an inexpensive hotel which had no elevator. He reasoned that a room was preferable to a residence with cooking facilities because he hated to cook. Propinquity of and accessibility to eating places with reasonable prices (he ate only two meals a day to save money) and the neighborhood social-club bar were most important. He preferred expending his air in getting to and from the cafe rather than at cooking and keeping up an apartment. A goodly amount of oxygen was expended at the bar, as he aptly put it, "shooting the breeze with the guys." The social-club bar was also important for financial reasons and for recruiting mobility assistants. The bartender and the patrons had known him for many years and knew his credit was good. This enabled him to get an occasional drink on credit, borrow money from friends, as well as enlist the aid of his friends with cars for especially difficult mobility situations.

When life conditions change as the disease progresses, mobility needs and residential locations are altered also.

For example, an elderly patient who lived most of his life in a downtown hotel, after several acute respiratory episodes and subsequent lung reserve decrease preferred to live downtown because of territorial familiarity and high propinquity to public transportation and eating places. He was also able to continue living alone by enlisting the aid of an elderly sister who served as an energy and money saver: she handled his personal laundry, ran errands, and invited him each week to Sunday dinner. A major change was locating himself in a moderately expensive hotel which had 24-hour clerks. The latter were important as interceptors of SOS signals should he require immediate medical attention. Such clerks are also important because they become familiar with a tenant's daily routines and consequently check on the tenant when there are changes in them.

Events such as razing an apartment, for urban redevelopment, where a patient has several tenant mobility assistants, or loss of mobility agents due to illness and death, can create difficulties not only in mobilization, but problems in balancing and juggling BMRs as well.

> For example, an elderly man who lived for many years in an economical boarding house operated by an interested and concerned landlady, and where he was on friendly terms with long-term boarders, was able to manage well on his limited BMRs. Unfortunately, the landlady developed severe arthritis so that she could no longer continue running the boarding house, putting the house up for sale. The closing of the house, and the loss of the landlady, meant he could not find comparable housing within his financial means, as well as the leading to the loss of his major mobility assistants and his major source of sociability—the landlady and fellow boarders.

ROUTING: PROCESS AND STRATEGIES

The process by which all persons, whether ill or healthy, deal with problems of mobility is by routing. The dimensions involved are: 1) anticipation of the number and types of activities in terms of available BMRs; 2) judgements whether to delete or postpone some activities, or to condense activities by combining several activities; 3) sequential ordering of activities in terms of importance, distance, time and energy involved in each activity, as well as anticipation of possible obstacles.

The degree of efficiency depends on both the mode of routing (own legs, public transportation, own car, other people's cars) and the degree of control over the mode of routing. Efficiency also depends on how much of other people's time is involved in completing an activity. One can condense activities in the shortest time when there is: 1) good control over the mode of routing; 2) control over the sequence and time involved for activities—such as having a prior appointment; and 3) sufficient energy. In situations where a person has little or no control over the mode of routing, efficiency nevertheless may be attained by stringent control of sequence, or expending more energy to hasten the routing process by running and generally in moving fast.

An emphysema patient's anticipation and planning of his route is essential to avoid the consequences of overexertion and anxiety. For example, Mr. P. lives on the second floor: before venturing outside he carefully plans for taking all the necessary paraphernalia and errand lists, and gauges the time and energy required to get to the bus stop. If late for the bus, he cannot run to catch it. Patients state than when they have forgotton a grocery list, drug prescription, form to take to the social worker, or whatever—then they find themselves getting anxious. Their anxiety is due in part to irritation with themselves, but also to their anticipation of having to make the trip back home or worse still climbing the stairs again.

The degree of planning for an ordinary activity (shopping for groceries) becomes long and complicated. A patient lives on the second floor. He must "recoup" oxygen after walking a single block even if on flat terrain. The grocery store is uphill, so after half a block he needs to rest in order to get his breath back. If he chats with the grocer then he needs to rest for the trip back home. If he carries a bag of groceries that means still more oxygen expenditure; so, even though the route home is downhill, he can only go ¾ of the block before becoming winded. Then at home he has a flight of stairs with which to contend. Twelve steps is his usual oxygen supply. With the extra grocery weight he requires "getting his wind back" every six to eight steps. What normals can do in twenty minutes is stretched out to one hour or more.

When a patient lacks money and therefore has little control over mode of routing, he may use his time as his major mobility resource: he expends small amounts of energy over an extended period of time. He may take the roundabout bus route to avoid a difficult terrain, even though a more direct route is possible. For example, to avoid a steep terrain he will walk downhill to catch a bus. After taking care of his business he transfers to two buses to catch a third bus which stops uphill from his house. Another patient's most direct route to the clinic involved walking across a wide thoroughfare with heavy traffic which he could not manage without running out of breath. He managed his routing by taking a time-consuming roundabout bus route which crossed the unmanageable thoroughfare.

An important routing concern which they all face is to find appropriate ways to "recoup" oxygen via locating appropriate "puffing" stations (another descriptive term used by a patient). Sitting down is the preferred way to "get the wind back," but such sitting places are seldom available in public. So the prevalent strategy is to start recouping oxygen while still able to stand. Sitting down on a street curb can cause a public scene. Moreover, in skid row or tenderloin areas one might get mistaken for a drunk. A wall, telephone pole, or mail box to lean against are considered good puffing stations. They have stated they do not venture downtown to shop because of the lack of appropriate puffing stations. One shopped exclusively at a particular department store because if its easy accesibility to the ladies lounge.

Emphysema patients must also weigh the weather more carefully than do normals because they must avoid catching colds. Windy weather is said to increase their breathing problems. Also there is the question of avoiding a tailwind or headwind. And, of course, smog greatly increases their breathing problems.

They must also anticipate other unforeseen obstacles. For example, patients living in deteriorated areas of the city where there are many predators tend not to venture outside too often. Should they be accosted they cannot run nor do they have the air to yell for help.

Whether sick or well, all people have varying daily, weekly, and monthly routing routines: routing to work, shop, pick up the cleaning, visit grandma, and so on. With their difficulties in routing and in the face of a scarcity of money, emphysema patients must be especially careful in planning their daily and weekly routing. Not infrequently those who live in difficult terrains (such as the second or third floor) plan so as to avoid unnecessary stair climbing. Thus a man who ate all his meals out planned his daily route so that once downstairs for breakfast he delayed climbing the stairs until after supper. This of course required locating stations, such as coffee shops and park benches for resting and killing time. Another patient who did her own cooking had an every-other-day route to the grocery store. This not only gave a change from her dingy apartment, but enabled her to socialize with the grocer and her neighborhood acquaintances. Also, her every-other-day shopping meant the grocery weight was more manageable than a large once-a-week shopping.

The daily and weekly expenditure of energy for routing must be planned so that on days which require an increased energy output (cleaning the apartment), routing for shopping is not done. A normal lunger would scarcely consider routing as necessary for getting dressed in the morning or for doing ordinary things around the house: they tend to think of routing only when great distances are involved. To illustrate the striking degree of daily routing required for emphysema patients:

> One lady who became short of breath after a few stops required two to three hours to get dressed. She arises from bed and goes to the bathroom, rests, washes by sitting in a chair but taking frequent rest periods in between, walks back to the bedroom, rests, and dresses with frequent rest periods.

> Another patient who mops his kitchen floor every week worked out an elaborate routing pattern. He gathers the cleaning paraphernalia and puts it near a chair in the middle of the room—all of which requires frequent periods of "getting my breath back." He mops a few strokes and rests, sitting in the chair.

With advanced emphysema, *all* activities require extremely careful routing. The routing is not only specific weekly and daily, but is also hourly, since extended rest periods are necessary after increased expenditure of energy. It is interesting to note that when making arrangements for interviews, patients not only specified certain days but times of the day such as—"Come in the morning around ten because I'll be too tired to talk in the afternoon," or "Come by in the afternoon because I rest after lunch and will be less tired."

MEDICAL REGIMEN AND MOBILITY

Whether a patient does or does not comply to his prescribed regimen and how he complies are determined in part by how the regimen interferes with his life style and mobility needs. In part, it also depends upon how be comprehends or miscomprehends the uses and effects of therapy.

Sometimes a patient's condition warrants extended inhalation therapy. These treatments may require daily visits to an outpatient clinic, or inhalation equipment instead may be sent to the home. Where daily visits are required, patients may not see their value considering the amount of time and energy required to get to the clinic. When respirators have been sent to their residence, that well-intentioned help by health personnel may not be perceived as helpful. Inhalation therapy is often ordered 2-3 times a day: This means that patients who live in difficult terrains, such as on the second floor, must plan to avoid frequent climbing of stairs. In order to avoid maneuvering the stairs several times a day, these patients confine themselves to their rooms. This often depresses them. The inhalation therapy does not improve their mobility; rather it immobilizes them. In fact, several patients thought inhalation therapy was a big nuisance and requested the doctor to discontinue the therapy.

Sometimes drugs via aerosol spray may be prescribed to immediately relieve periodic respiratory distress. These drugs may be ordered at most 3-6 times a day because of undesirable side effects.[5] When an activity requires extended oxygen expenditure there is likelihood of drug overdose, since these sprays provide extra needed energy to complete an activity. One patient patted his portable nebulizer, stating it was his "life saver" as it gave him the needed extra spurt of energy in difficult routing situations. Although he had been warned by the physician about overdosing, unfortunately he did not know what were the symptoms of overdose.

Also, although broncho-dilator drugs help breathing, these frequently cause untoward side effects such as nervousness and sleeplessness. Sometimes sedatives are required to counteract these side effects, but such drugs may leave the patient groggy. Not infrequently, balancing of the two drugs can become a problem. An imbalance may mean a patient has no energy to be mobile because he lacks sleep, or is too groggy to get around. When health personnel are not attentive to the patient's drug balance problems, he may doubt both the usefulness of the therapy and the competence of his physician.

Patients' criteria of therapeutic effectiveness are based on how well the therapies help them to be mobile in their daily movements. They may omit a drug to see how much difference this makes, as did a man whose daily route included a walk to the park. He tested the therapy by the ease or dis-ease not only in his walking there, but in how he managed the park's various terrains. Such criteria are in contrast to those used by professionals which involve elaborate laboratory tests, or reflected in the inaccurate standards found in patients' medical charts: "gets short of breath after 1 block, 2 blocks, etc."

One of the more disheartening facts uncovered by the interviewing of these patients was the neglect of teaching rehabilitation measures to patients; such as respiratory exercises, respiratory hygiene, and conditioning him to breathe more efficiently. On the current emphysema medical scene, the emphasis has been primarily on the acute respiratory episode treated in acute care facilities. The outcome of such unbalanced emphasis has been heroic efforts to mobilize the patients, but no real assistance in achieving effective mobilization for living once the acute episode is over.

REFERENCES

1. The pathological changes result in decreased oxygen supply due to decreased lung compliance, decreased diffusion capacity, and increased airway resistance. Hollis G. Boren, "Pulmonary emphysema: clinical and physiological aspects," from Gerald L. Baum (ed.), *The Textbook of Pulmonary Diseases,* Boston: Little, Brown and Co., 1965, pp. 421-447; S. M. Farber and R. H. Wilson, Pulmonary Emphysema, *Clinical Symposium* (Ciba), 20:2, 1968.

2. "Recouping" oxygen supply is not an accurate physiological term, but a term to describe the breathing problem used by one patient interviewed.

3. Donald L. Dudley, et al., "Dyspnea: physiologic and psychologic observations," *J. Psychosomatic Res.,* 11:325, 1968.

4. Donald L. Dudley, et al., "Long-term adjustment, prognosis and death in irreversible obstructive pulmonary emphysema," *Psychosomatic Med.,* 31:510, 1969.

5. William Sawyer Eisenstadt, "Some observations on a new syndrome—respiratory medicamentosa," *Ann. Allergy,* 27:188-190, 1969.

CHAPTER 13

CHRONIC RENAL FAILURE
AND THE PROBLEM OF FUNDING*

BARBARA SUCZEK

Chronic renal failure inevitably involves its victims in a dual crisis: physical and financial. Because the functions performed by the kidneys are absolutely necessary to survival, the patient must be put on a dialysis machine, through which his blood is filtered. This regimen 1) is extremely expensive, both financially and temporally; 2) must be repeated at regular and frequent intervals (usually two or three times a week); and, 3) must be ongoing (because the kidney function is absolutely essential to the life process, there can be no surcease from the need for mechanical intervention except through kidney transplant, a solution itself fraught with physical and financial problems—or death).

Since there can be little or no reasonable hope for relief from the burden of heavy and continuous expense, some extraordinary source of funds must be located. The alternatives are: 1) *self-funding*, whereby the patient is able to provide for himself from his personal assets; 2) *private funding*, either through some business arrangement (such as individual or group health insurance) or through charitable contributions—personal or organizational; 3) *public funding*, through any of various governmental agencies; or 4) *no funding*, in which case the patient does not locate a source of funds and dies for lack of treatment.

Of these alternatives, the fourth—*no funding*—is still the most prevalent (as will be discussed below). The first—*self-funding*—requires a level of income and/or personal assets so far in excess of national averages as to render it a negligible role in the overall funding drama. Except, perhaps, in such instances as might involve persons of advanced age who have substantial personal savings and otherwise light living expenses, the prospect of a lifetime on dialysis raises serious funding problems for all but the most spectacularly affluent.[1] Almost by definition, the chronic renal failure patient is a person entangled in a fund-raising struggle whose double objective is to pay for life-sustaining care while averting

*This case is a shortened version of an unpublished paper; another version was published in Society 10:40-49, 1973. The case is based on information obtained during 2 years of fieldwork and interviews in Northern California. Patients, physicians, nurses, unit administrators, social workers, and financial administrators are among those who were interviewed and sometimes observed.

personal financial wipeout: a deadly game of financial dodgeball played while simultaneously wrestling with problems of insufficient time and physical debility.

Under such conditions funding becomes an ongoing preoccupation, with dramatic force sufficient to compel the behavior not only of the patient and possibly his kin but often of the professional personnel involved in his treatment as well.

REALIZING THE PROBLEM

In the overall funding process there are two steps that are logically prior to the actual acquisition and dispersal of funds. These are: (1) realization of the dimensions of the problem and (2) assessment of available resources. The first step involves astonishingly complex considerations.

The patient

Although informed awareness is an essential step in the effective budgeting of resources, the dimensions of the financial problem confronting the victim of chronic renal failure may be difficult for him to realize for several reasons. The foremost is the ambiguity—etiological, diagnostic, and prognostic—of the disability itself. Whether or not the affected individual has had prior warning either of the possibility or the probability of kidney failure, the actual moment of total functional collapse seems to be only grossly predictable. Irreversible kidney failure can occur so gradually that it is almost imperceptible, or so abruptly— sometimes with no previous warning whatsoever—that it manifests itself in a major physical crisis requiring heroic measures to save the patient's life. In either case the effect is to obscure the financial problem. When crises occur, rarely are they manifested in such a way and at such a time in the disease career that the patient has an opportunity to evaluate the situation for himself in order to decide whether, all things considered, he wishes to commit himself to the heavy burdens of a dialyzed future or to elect death instead. Thus he is apt to find himself in a position of *fait accompli* from which, for a number of reasons, it may be difficult to extricate himself. The net effect is to bind the patient—at least initially—to life-sustaining effort, an effort that will inevitably direct his steps to the treadmill of funding. It is a direction, however, that is rarely of the patient's conscious choosing and its consequences are not often calculated.

The medical staff

Usually the physician bears the ethical burden of life-and-death decisions. To relieve some of the onus of such fateful responsibility, physicians have official guidelines and collegial committees whom they can consult for support. Such guidelines are customarily cast in terms of medical and psychological concepts and relate primarily to psychomedical evaluation of the patient's condition, aside from problems immediately attributable to the kidney failure.

This is not to say, however, that the financial condition of the patient will have no bearing on whether or not he will be rescued from a physical crisis. There can be little doubt that, unofficially, decisions to rescue will reflect judgments of social worth, and assessment of a patient's financial condition may be a factor that is indirectly involved in the overall calculus. The issue is a sensitive one, since to save life according to ability to pay is contrary to overt medical, social, and psychological values. Institutionalized moral reprehension, by discouraging candor, may therefore obscure the dimensions of the financial problem, questions of funding being relegated to a position of secondary and somewhat unworthy consideration. Thus, the link, if any, between the rescue decision and the patient's financial condition is apt to be swept under the rug where it is, for all practical purposes, invisible.

Additional considerations

Other difficulties impede the realization of financial needs. 1) The physician, guided by a widespread belief that mental attitude affects physical welfare, may be reluctant to divulge depressing details that could be seen as potentially threatening to the patient's will to survive. 2) Many patients resist bad news about their conditions, refusing to accept the implications of available information if such information is threatening. 3) The patient may be unable to comprehend the physician's medical terminology and scientific frame of reference with a corresponding failure on the part of the physician to understand what it is that the patient has not understood. 4) There may be confusion about who should be the informing agent. Thus, information may be garnered piecemeal from a variety of sources: the doctor, the nursing staff, case workers, other patients, medical folklore, fortuitously in the course of reading, or through deliberate personal research. 5) The family doctor, who may know the patient and his circumstances at first hand, may be relatively unaware of the physical and financial implications of his ailment, whereas the specialist, who may understand the latter, will quite likely be unacquainted with the personal problems of his patient.

Thus, regardless of his economic or class status, the patient—sick and worried—is forced to chart a perilous physical and financial course through an apparently indifferent sea. It is an unfortunate fact that the physically healthy lack—as a rule—the imagination, the time, and the emotional energy to sustain for long any deep involvement with seemingly interminable medical problems. Bolstered by a proud but largely unexamined assumption that "we," as Americans, are probably doing as well as can be expected in providing for general health care, the chronically sick and those intimately involved with their care are essentially left to take their own soundings.

ASSESSING RESOURCES

Sooner or later the need for financial assessment will arrive. The point at which the kidney failure is pronounced *chronic*—the point at which it becomes clear to the patient that his survival depends, henceforth, on hemodialysis—is usually the moment of financial truth. This is because an insistent new dimension has been added to the patient's life: he has entered into a partnership with a machine. Above all, the machine is a greedy and inexorable consumer of time and money.

The assessment of resources is not a simple, direct process. There is, on the one hand, the problem of what resources are available and, on the other, the matter of whether or not availability is perceived. Actual availability of specific funding sources is usually contingent upon criteria that define membership, either categorically ascribed or based on voluntary association. Of the former, *age* is frequently a determinant. Persons under twenty-one, for example, may qualify for assistance from funds for crippled children; those selected for dialysis who are over sixty-five have access to Medicare. Groups may also provide funding possibilities: membership in group insurance plans, for example, or in religious and fraternal organizations. A sense of group responsibility often leads to united effort to raise funds to assist a stricken fellow member. Affiliation is useful in the struggle to stay alive.

While membership in particular categories or groups may give access to special funds, individuals are not necessarily aware of this. A general lack of coordinated information contributes to the overall sense of chaos that seems to pervade the funding of chronic renal failure. This is true of the scene in general as well as within specific organizations. Unions, for example, even though they may negotiate carefully formulated health insurance coverage, rarely, if ever, provide for trained personnel to interpret the terms of their policies for their individual members.

TREADING THE FUNDING MILL

Two major phases in the illness trajectory are each accompanied by special funding problems. These are an acute, or *rescue* period and a chronic, or *prolonged maintenance* period. Since the latter phase may extend over an entire lifetime, it will almost certainly be accompanied by a sequential depletion of funding sources—each failure initiating a new crisis propelling most patients into search for new funds.

Exhaustion of funds and the subsequent search for new sources is a condition of life for the patient. The ultimate available recourse, other than death, is to public funds. Such a solution may, however, be conditional upon the patient's being reduced to a literal state of pauperization,[2] an alternative desperately to be avoided as long as hope for a more dignified solution remains. As a result, fund-raising takes on the quality of running on a treadmill. A successful kidney transplant may seem the only real hope for escape. Such an escape, unfortunately, involves massive problems of its own, such as locating donors, the inevitable surgical risks, and the possibility of organ rejection. It is also an expensive procedure. If successful, there is hope for genuine relief at the economic as well as the physical level. If unsuccessful, the patient returns to the treadmill.

Funding the rescue period

Although the costs of the rescue period will probably be higher than those of subsequent phases of the illness, the initial blow is typically cushioned by health insurance. It is estimated that approximately 80 percent of dialysis patients carry some sort of major medical coverage at the time of the onset of illness. However, health insurance policies are primarily geared to protect the insured against the cost of acute illness; they are rarely adequate for coping with the long-term financial drain associated with chronic illness.

One problem, however, is that the claimant may be simply and overwhelmingly ignorant about the terms of his insurance. It is a rare person who has the slightest idea what his insurance can, in fact, be expected to cover or what such coverage would mean, in any event, within the context of a specific illness trajectory. Nor does it seem possible that the situation could be otherwise. There is simply no way for the individual to be able to anticipate all eventualities and their consequences. Who, for example, could have guessed a few years ago that even "forever" might be barely adequate as a time stipulation? Yet this is only a slight overstatement of what has become a fact of life for thousands of victims of renal failure. Thus, a policy carrying a $20,000 liability limitation may seem, to the healthy, more than adequate to protect a family from the costs of even major illnesses. However, in the case of one young woman—a wife and mother—who was stricken with kidney failure, $13,000 of such a policy was consumed in less than four months and it covered, even so, only 80 percent of her overall medical expense. Thus, the family was already more than $2,000 out of pocket, the insurance was 65 percent depleted and there was still a lifetime of expense ahead which, for a woman of 27, might be expected to extend for upwards of fifty years. For this young and previously prospering family, a carefully planned insurance program literally melted away, carrying with it many of their hopes and plans for the future. Unfortunately *this was not an unusual case.* Among renal failure patients and their families, such experiences are common.

Ignorance of content is often accompanied by ignorance of procedure. For patients who are unfamiliar with the intricacies of bureaucratic paperwork or for those who are too sick to concern themselves with it, filling out the required forms according to prescribed time schedules may present an almost insurmountable problem.

In the whole "system," there seems to be no one, anywhere, assigned a role whose primary function is to help the patient understand and order his financial affairs strictly in accordance with his own needs and interests. The usual procedure followed by insured patients seems to be that of submitting claims on an *ad hoc* basis until such time as payment is refused. If refusal is based on a technicality, a running dispute with the company may ensue. If refusal is based on the fact that the company's liability is spent—that the source of funds is exhausted—a new crisis is precipitated. Although a crisis is often plainly foreseeable, rarely does one find a patient who has made any advance plans for dealing with it. "I just don't know *what* I'll do when the insurance runs out!" is a typical comment. This unpreparedness is undoubtedly because there are few—terrifyingly few—available options. The patient, helpless and bewildered, simply drifts into crisis, hoping that, when the point is reached, some solution sufficient unto the day will present itself.

Prolonged maintenance funding

In the prolonged maintenance period the patient's condition—physical and financial—has usually been somewhat stabilized. Although the problem of keeping the body chemistry in balance is never perfectly solved, the physical condition is basically under control and so there is some opportunity for predicting and planning the funding of future needs. However, the period is characterized by a series of funding crises.

How early and to what extent an individual will experience the treadmill effect of the prolonged maintenance period hinges on many contingencies. Employment status is a major consideration. It makes a critical difference, for example, whether a patient is financially dependent, self-supporting, or the breadwinner for a family. Although there are problems associated with various financially dependent roles—the mother of a family, for example, often must make arrangements for long periods of child-care and her household tasks must somehow be accomplished when she, herself, is physically unable to cope with them—the greatest difficulty is usually occasioned when it is incumbent upon the afflicted person to earn a living.

This is because: 1) The time needed for dialysis may cut seriously into working hours. 2) Physical debility not only hampers productivity and overall efficiency but also limits the sorts of work that can be undertaken. Occupational careers that involve a considerable outlay of physical energy, or require extensive travelling, for example, may have to be abandoned. 3) It may be difficult to find any sort of suitable work since employment policies are frequently conjoined with insurance regulations that will, almost certainly, reject persons suffering from serious chronic disease.

Early retirement is a frequent solution among those whose age and seniority status permit them that alternative. The person who can retire on a pension and is qualified to receive help from Medicare is in a relatively good financial position, providing there are not extraneous complicating factors. Under other circumstances, however, retirement may be an extremely threatening matter. Take, for example, the plight of a man who had reached the compulsory retirement age but whose wife—twenty years his junior—was on hemodialysis that was being funded through his occupational insurance.

The issue of state financed medical help is fraught, in some states, with bitterness and altercation, and the financing of renal failure—because of its chronicity and its extraordinarily high cost—is a particularly touchy focal point. There are three sources of major dispute: welfare restrictions, governmental responsibility, and administrative red tape.

Welfare restrictions. To qualify for funds from MediCal, the patient (in a state like California) must divest himself of any personal property or income he may have in excess of that permitted to recipients of state welfare. The MediCal plan is apparently so designed in order to insure that the individual will not free-load at the taxpayers' expense—he will assume liability and share the cost of his illness. In operation it is like a deductible clause based on the patient's income. A single person, for example, with an income of $500 a month may be permitted a maintenance need allowance of $110 a month: income above that amount must be used for medical expenses before MediCal will intervene in his behalf. In addition, MediCal will not assist anyone who owns cash or property in excess of a value of $1,200 (personal dwelling excepted) and/or cash value of life insurance over $100 per dependent. Thus, if the patient has been fortunate enough or foresighted enough to provide some security for his family, he is expected to see to the dispersal of that security before he can apply to MediCal for the funds needed to save his life. Once reduced to the welfare level, there seems little likelihood that a patient can find the means to regain his independence.

To many patients and professionals, the situation seems not only unfortunate but contrary to American principles and goals. It is a commonly expressed fear that such prescriptions are generating a "welfare race" of persons who no longer have any incentive to self-help. There is also a prevailing sense of injustice that a victim of illness through no perceivable fault of his own should be thus reduced to such an apparently punitive plight.

Administrative red tape. The organization and distribution of state health care funds is apparently so tangled in a web of duplication, evasion, and conflicting purpose that the overall result is mass confusion. Presumably the outgrowth of legislative ambivalence, the present situation seems to be characterized by overlapping jurisdiction, conflict of policy, bureaucratic shuffling of responsibility, and a general lack of coordination and accountability.

Loopholing. This is an informal device whereby officially proscribed actions may be unofficially redefined in terms that permit their accomplishment without open infraction of rules. There is considerable evidence to suggest that—even as lack of clear definition in the private insurance transaction sometimes leads to exploitable loopholes—confusion and ambiguity at the state level inadvertently leaves gaps whereby patients may escape some of the more devastating effects of eligibility rulings.

Because loopholing must, of necessity, be evasive in method as well as in goal, it entails some special problems to dialysis patients. The medical staff or a case worker may point out the possibility of making "paper statements" that will indicate intent but may not be binding in actual commission. Such patterns of evasion are unlikely to be explicitly stated but will probably be couched, themselves, in evasive terms as a protection against the danger of legal and political repercussions.

> . . . The social workers can't say right out what is going on. They have to hope the patients will catch on when they say things like, "Well, in your case I wouldn't worry too much." Once in a while, but not very often, they'll just come right out with it. But this is dangerous.

Awkwardness can stem from the fact that an individual who is unsophisticated in tactical loopholing may overlook or misunderstand the functional possibilities embodied therein, or else be strongly offended by what he may view as fundamental impropriety. Some persons take loopholing easily in stride, seeing it in the light of a sensible and innocuous business arrangement—like maneuvering all possible personal advantages from income tax regulations—or as a more-or-less empty ritualistic gesture: a mindless genuflexion. Others view it as simple dishonesty and suffer accordingly—either because desperation leads them to comply with evasionary tactics against the dictates of their scruples, in which case they suffer from the demeaning pangs of bad conscience, or because they do not, and bear in consequence the effects of financial anguish.

Loopholing can sometimes be accomplished by making a change in legal status (a device not infrequently employed by the urban poor). For instance, a social worker remarked that:

> The husband, who was the patient, was in his fifties but he had a young family from a second marriage. . . . It was a working class family: the mother had a job as a salesgirl and he was a garage attendant. When they applied for MediCal, the welfare guidelines for a family of their size were just impossible—if they kept their combined income they would be just working for the state. It was a total mess! Well, the upshot of the matter was that after he had been on dialysis for a month, the marriage broke up. They got a divorce. It was the only way to save the income. . . . The woman continued to take care of him and was obviously very fond of him.

To be successful, loopholing usually depends upon an alliance of various participants: patient, case worker, eligibility worker, for example. If these do not share understandings of need or definitions of loyalty the situation may dissolve into one of personal rancor and agency infighting, with counter attributions of bureaucratic inhumanity and fiscal irresponsibility being hurled back and forth, to the apparent benefit of no one.

The patient, having at this point in his funding career exhausted, in all likelihood, whatever meager resources he may have had available to him, stands more or less helpless to act in his own behalf. He is like a prisoner at the bar waiting for the result of adversary action to decide his fate: a negative decision will condemn him to the humiliation and distress of ultimate financial wipe-out.

Choosing death. Probably there is a significantly higher incidence of suicidal behavior among chronic renal failure patients than for the population at large, or even as compared with other chronic disease contexts. Suicidal behavior refers both to deliberate action taken by the patient to terminate his own life and to his refusal to undergo or to cooperate in treatment with an intent to accomplish the same end.

Considerable attention has been directed to identifying the predisposing psychological factors that may contribute to the self-destructive impulse. Properties attributed to the patient—such as ego strength and self-esteem—have been defined and measured as independent variables controlling the suicidal tendency. Unresolved dependency conflicts have been posited as contributory—if not causal—factors in the suicidal despair of many renal failure patients, being directly related to the aggravating problem of machine bondage. Undoubtedly this is an important and authentic area of research and such findings are difficult—and perhaps, impossible—to refute. However, given the reality of the present, it does not seem always necessary to look—for motivation—to the past. Given, for example, the circumstances of financial treadmilling and its dread terminus of financial wipeout and hopeless economic dependency with inevitable concomitants of poverty, insecurity, erosion of personal autonomy and loss of privacy, such problems as may be related to machine dependency seem considerably diminished in importance.

Self-esteem and ego strength, moreover, are personal properties whose possession may contribute equally as well to a decision in favor of altruistic suicide as to a determination to live. The conditioning effect that circumstance and status can exert on the direction of personal decision is demonstrated in the following two examples. The first is as reported by the administrator of a dialysis center:

> There are lots of cases where patients just haven't showed up. Patients have been referred to private centers, say, where they demand a deposit of $10,000, and they just toss in the towel. One man I know of personally—thirty-seven years of age with three children and $19,000 in the bank—elected to die. He was perfectly frank. He said if he went into treatment he would destroy his family.

Another patient—a twenty-two year old Asian, the father of two young children—faced a different situation and, in accordance with his perception of it, reached a different decision:

> . . . The way I see it, I'm going to be in the hole all my life. I worry about bills. I worry about a change in the laws that will cut off what we're getting now. Most of my worry is money. . . . It's my kids. They're forcing me to stay alive. I keep seeing myself caring for them until they're on their own. I imagine what it will be like for them if I die. They'll hardly have anything. My wife didn't even finish high school and she wouldn't be able to take care of them. . . . They'd hardly get anything to eat, maybe. The thought keeps me going. I want to live . . .

In neither of these cases did the patient—by demeanor or behavior—manifest lack of self-esteem or neurotic fear of dependency. Opposite decisions were apparently reached according to real differences in external conditions.

RECOMMENDATIONS

There are a number of recommendations of varying degrees of practicability whose institution might somewhat alleviate the distress of chronic renal failure patients. These range from suggestions relating to comparatively minor read-justments to those of a scope that would require fundamental changes in policy and in administrative organization. For instance:

1) Since it is financially inexpedient to tie insurance reimbursement to requirements for in-service treatment, insurance carriers should abandon practices of outpatient stepchilding.

2) Unions should institute a policy of assigning specifically trained persons to the task of advising their members, on an individual basis, concerning the interpretation and execution of their insurance affairs.

3) Providers should work together to coordinate services in order to relieve expensive duplication and overlap that often result when efforts are basically competitive.

4) Dialysis centers should be operated on a twenty-four hour basis.

5) Health personnel should be trained in hemodialysis techniques in order to assist home care patients, if not on a regular, at least on an emergency basis.

6) Prepaid transportation service should be provided for center-based patients: urban, suburban, and interurban.

7) Some relaxation should be made in insurance policies in order to encourage organizations and business to employ chronically ill individuals to the extent that the volition and physical capabilities of such persons allow them to work.

8) State health insurance policies and their administration should be reorganized: (a) to remove health care assistance from the restrictions of welfare eligibility rules; (b) to streamline administration by eliminating redundant, expensive, and absurd red-tape formalities; (c) to coordinate agency policies in such a way that providers can have some reasonable basis for predicting the time and extent of reimbursement for services rendered.

The implementation of any or all such suggestions would, almost certainly, bring some measure of relief to the individual patient. It would not, however, eliminate the basic problem and the crisis-to-crisis course of the funding process would continue with, at best, its pace slightly abated.

The basic problem is that the cost of preserving the life of the renal failure patient eventually exceeds the ability of any individual to pay for it—from his own pocket or from privately available resources. If he is to survive, therefore, the chances are that he must, in the end, be subsidized or supported by public funds. It is an eventuality that occurs through no fault of his own: he is not responsible for his illness; he is not to blame for the exorbitancy of its costs; there is virtually no way that, by exercise of proper character and foresight, he might have been able to stave off financial need. Yet he is subjected to restrictions that suggest that—in exchange for public help—he has incurred an expiatory obligation to live, together with his dependents, at a level of penitential poverty.

REFERENCES

1. Since the expense involved—both initial and ongoing—is in a state of flux and circumstantially variable, any estimate can only be a rough approximation. At this writing (1972) the figure for center-based care in California has been given at anywhere from $10,000 to $40,000 a year. This figure does not, in all likelihood, include professional fees. Home-based dialysis, subsequent to the training period, runs from $2,500 to $7,000 a year. (Items such as emergency hospital care, physical checkups, and the like, may be but are not necessarily included in these estimates. The fact that there is no generally agreed upon stipulation as to what items should be included in such a statement means that the figures are not usefully comparable.) None of these estimates takes into consideration such subsidary expenses as travel, nor loss of income due to impaired ability to work.

2. As probably in many states, in California recipients of medical and of welfare funds are legally bound by property restrictions. Severe limitations are placed on what can be owned and earned or collected from other sources of income. Existence can be maintained only at the poverty level. Ideologically oriented to discourage abuse of public funds by the lazy and unambitious, it is difficult to see how the stringency of such guidelines can possibly be construed as similarly useful in the case of the chronically ill.

CHAPTER 14

DYING IN HOSPITALS*

BARNEY GLASER AND ANSELM STRAUSS

HOSPITAL OR HOME

The choice of where to end the patient's trajectory hinges on how staff, family, and patient wish it to be managed during the last hours. The choice involves not only physical environment and equipment; it also determines which persons are to preside over the final stage of dying, and the death itself. If the patient is moved, management is, in effect, redelegated. Staff may, for example, redelegate management to the family, possibly providing some equipment or a special nurse. Or the family may delegate management to the hospital.

A patient's earlier dying may have been viewed as a situation calling largely for routine care, whether at home or in the hospital. But the ultimate dying evokes special values and special problems that bear upon how staff, family, and patient consider and relate to each other in deciding where, with whom, and how the patient shall encounter death. Where the person dies becomes the context of what many people consider a special occasion—his death. . . .

Family

The basic issue confronting the family in deciding where the patient is to die is how they want his last hours to be managed. This issue in turn raises the problem of who should manage these hours to achieve their desires. In considering these two issues, several aspects of the last hours are relevant. "How" includes questions of managing the patient's medical care, of maintaining his physical and psychological comfort, of the possibility of unduly prolonging his life, of the possibility of imposing an excessive burden on the home, of the relative financial costs at home or hospital, and of proper disposal of his body. The problem of "who" will be in charge, either at home or in the hospital, requires consideration of many questions: Will they allow proper ceremonies during the last hours? Will they allow close friends and relatives to be with the patient, or will

*From Time for dying, Chicago, 1965, Aldine Publishing Co.

the patient probably die alone or with unfamiliar people in unfamiliar surroundings? Will the people present at the death bed be able to take the emotional burden? Whether the family actually considers these issues at all (quite aside from whether they consider them "realistically") varies greatly; sometimes there is no time, sometimes the staff alone make and enforce the decisions, or there is no interest.

Prolonging the patient's life is a crucial consideration for family members when deciding where the patient should die. In America, a hospital death means yielding to the staff virtually complete control over his care. The hospital is equipped for the fight for life, which may impose undue or unnecessary prolonging. But some family members may want every last-ditch effort made. They wish to be able to say to themselves and others that everything that medical science could do was actually done literally "until the very end." Some families feel so strongly about this last effort at prolonging that they send the patient to the hospital even when it is unlikely he will get there alive. In their minds, the "right thing" for the patient is a hospital career at the end of his trajectory.

Some families, however, feel that the sacrifice of a few days or hours of life is a reasonable exchange for the opportunity to die at home. In "Ezio's Last Days,"[1] the wife of Ezio Pinza, the famous singer, tells of making such a decision about her husband. Mrs. Pinza had a few hours to decide how and with whom her husband's last hours would be spent. As is typical in such situations, she consulted with a relative and a trusted friend. Both agreed "it would be best to leave Ezio in the peace and dignity of his own home." She almost consulted her oldest child, but felt she was too young for the burden of such a "tragic decision." She then asked her husband, who could not talk but could shake his head; the answer was to stay at home. Mrs. Pinza then called Dr. Fogel and said, "Ezio remains at home." The doctor replied, "I think you have made the right decision. This I say as a friend and as his physician."

Thus the decision to keep the patient at home to die under familiar circumstances was made with the support of several others, including the patient himself. It took into careful consideration the fact that comforting medical care could be supplied as adequately at home as at the hospital. If comfort had been impossible at home, it is likely that the patient would have been sent to the hospital, even if prolonging was also an outcome.

Mrs. Pinza's situation was clear; her husband had only a short time before death. But sometimes the family members must take their option on hospital or home when it is less clear whether the hospital may possibly save the patient. The evidence may indicate that the likely outcome is a useless, costly prolonging, yet family members may not feel convinced and medical personnel in attendance cannot say. "Certainty" is, to be sure, perhaps as much a function of the person as of the evidence. In one such case, a father had a heart attack while hiking in the mountains. The decision fell on the son either to let him die while still pursuing his valued way of life or to try to get him to a hospital by helicopter. The chances were that the father would die on the way, or if he arrived alive at the hospital would simply be prolonged a few days. However, one doctor at the hospital could possibly save him with a new procedure. This slight chance was not enough for the son, and he let his father stay, with his wife, in familiar circumstances. He preferred to manage his father's death in a way befitting the way the father had lived, and to leave him in the company of the people whom he loved, rather than providing him a "heroics" career in a hospital. The emotional finesse of such situations is great indeed, for a decision not to send the patient to the hospital for a short prolonging is in effect a decision to let him die.

Once the decision has been made to let the patient die, the family members can exercise control over how he will die. This control is easier to vary and manage in the home than in the hospital because of the greater nonobservability of care given at home. . . .[T]he hospital staff is in most instances under various pressures to keep the patient alive. Only in infrequent situations of nonobservability do they help him die or provide a set-up for autoeuthanasia. In the home, the family or private duty nurse can easily be more "humane." They can refrain from rescue tactics or can easily discontinue life-sustaining medication or help the patient commit autoeuthanasia. Of course, any such decision is articulated with management of the temporal life of the family and friends present in the home. They cannot be expected to wait days when the patient might be conveniently dead within hours. The question is how best to manage the patient's death amidst these familiar circumstances at home. . . .

Financial considerations also enter into the family's decision about where to have the patient die. Although private medical insurance and Medicare have in recent years brought about drastic changes in the financial aspects of dying, it is still, for many families, less costly to have their relative die at home. Sometimes they can manage entirely by themselves, or with the help of a night nurse or a day-care "practical nurse." Neighbors may pitch in to help when, say, a mother must shop or work, but this generosity lasts only so long, and can easily run out before the constant watch maintained during the last hours. On the other hand, if the patient can die in a state or county hospital as a free patient, or on a health insurance plan, the family may find it financially advantageous to send him to the hospital for his last days, so that they do not have to hire home nursing care. . . .

In considering the problems of prolonging and finances, family members must take into account the burden of care that will fall on them if the patient spends his last hours at home. We have mentioned the problems of whether they can provide the necessary physical care and whether they can endure the death emotionally. Another problem is whether they have suitable space at home for him. Although the patient may have shared a room while in good health, usually it is preferable that he be segregated from the family while dying. If segregation is not practicable—as in small urban apartments or small houses—it may be too much of a burden to keep the patient at home during his last hours. His presence would be too pervasive, would dominate too much the lives that must go on while he dies. The space problem is especially difficult for the poor who live in cramped urban settings.

Other aspects that the families consider are how "humanely" they want the patient treated and what kinds of company and ceremonies they want for him. Americans, as we have said, by and large take it for granted that the hospital is the place to die; it is equipped to handle the medical burden of the last hours. It is mainly hospital staff members who wish the patient to die at home, if possible. But Americans also want hospital death to be "humane." Families express this wish in the common preference for retaining more social-psychological control over the patient's last hours, leaving to the staff the management of medical and nursing care. Family members want as much chance as possible to be with him, and want staff members to be more considerate of the social-psychological dimensions of staff relationships (such as talk, attention, and information) with the patient during his last hours. The family wants to be present during the last hours, be continually informed, hold the patient's hand, and talk with him.

In many hospital situations, however, kinsmen are put in a waiting room and are forbidden to be with their loved one at the end. They are told that their presence is too stressful for the patient, who "must rest" as he dies. But they are not told that their presence is likely to threaten the sentimental order of the ward, and so disrupt work. It might disturb the staff to see the family mourning with the patient; it might disturb other patients to witness scenes of what is possibly in store for them. If the family loses composure in public during these intense hours, then surely everyone will be upset. The staff's solution, most generally, is to let family members visit for short periods and remain in the waiting room as long as they like, but to suggest they go home for rest. Thus the probability is low that kinsmen will be with the patient at death, even if they are waiting just down the hall from him. Consequently, they will experience his death as an announcement, not a graceful passing.

In sum, Americans tend to accept the patient's death in the impersonal hospital, where "the ebb and flow of events is controlled by routine and by strangers," instead of at home, in familiar circumstances and among familiar people. Yet at the same time they wish more control over whom he is with and how his last hours with these people are socially managed. Kinsmen wish to make certain he dies with familiar company, if not surroundings not with strangers or alone, as is liable to happen in the hospital.

In Europe and Asia . . . families generally feel that the patient ought to die at home in familiar circumstances, in his own bed. So they accept, if they can manage the situation, the doctors' sending him home—or they just take him home. One reason for this stand is their wish to engage in ceremonies in conjunction with the patient's passing. Ceremonies—both religious and familial—have an important role in America, too, but they are arranged rather differently.

The family gathering at the patient's bedside is easier to handle at home, although there is always the problem of timing the gathering of kin with the death. However, at home the family can wait while doing other things, can easily gather periodically to chat with the patient, and can rush to his bedside when his time comes. This kind of gathering is especially appropriate for an aged parent or grandparent, but can occur for all family members, young and old. It is considered desirable in Asia, but in the United States tends to be overlooked or neglected in favor of having a few intimates next to the patient while he receives medical and nursing care in the hospital. At home, the family gathering can continue as a wake for the patient, which Asians prefer. In America, the family must go to the funeral parlor several hours after the death. As one family member said after a hospital death, "They won't even leave the poor body around long enough for a wake." In Asian and some European hospitals, there is likely to be a chapel or funeral room in which the family continue their gathering as a wake.

Provision for religious ceremonies is more or less standardized in American hospitals. As a patient nears death, some have a routine procedure for calling a chaplain of the correct faith. The problem for the staff is timing, for they may call the chaplain too late or too soon; either error upsets the family and patient. Staff also must be able to reach the chaplain in time. If the priest whom they usually call is unavailable, then they must find another one somewhere, and fast. Also, they are sometimes not certain of the religion of the patient if it is not marked on his record, or may not know if the patient or family wishes a particular form of last rites. The family may not be at hand, or the patient may be comatose. In the emergency ward, it is fairly often impossible to figure out what to do about a religious ceremony.

All in all, the American family in abdicating control to the hospital over the last hours does so knowing that the staff will arrange for religious ceremonies if necessary. In Asia and some European countries, the family will arrange for them in the hospital but prefers to have them at home, linked with the family gathering. The home is where ceremonies can be done "properly," to the comfort of the family as well as the patient.

Sometimes in the American hospital the sacraments are given to a sentient patient who did not know he was dying and whose family is not present. "This situation is enough to scare a patient to death," a chaplain in such a case told us. He was also distressed for another reason: "The thing that shook me is that she died so quickly, and I had more to say to her." Mistiming in the family's calling for the chaplain is more likely in the hospital than at home because they may not immediately learn of, or be able to observe, changes in the patient's condition. In the home, it is more feasible to alert the clergyman in advance and then have him call back frequently to inquire when he will be needed, thus forestalling delays and mistiming. He can then come in time to comfort the family and perform last rites. But this repeated calling is bothersome to staff in the hospital, and they are not too likely to give adequate information until they are ready to call the chaplain.

The family can make or participate in the decision of where the patient is to die only if they have the time and are given or take the opportunity to do so. Then they balance out the several factors we have discussed. While individual cases vary, the national patterns are clear enough. In the United States, it is increasingly unusual to have a patient at home for his death, but in Asia and in some European countries it is unusual to leave a patient in the hospital for his death.

The patient

For the patient, the basic issue about where to die is how he wishes it managed and with whom he wants to be. During the last hours many patients have no choice—they are dying too quickly, are comatose or not lucid enough to decide, or require hospital care that cannot be given at home. Some patients have no home or their kinsmen cannot take them. Some are not aware they are dying, and thus are denied a choice, even though they would prefer to die at home.

Several factors are typically involved in a patient's own decision to remain in the hospital. Even if he can leave the hospital, he may wish to stay because he expects the pain during the last hours to be great, and feels more sure of having a painless death in the hands of skilled staff members rather than a distressed family and a single nurse. Or the patient unable to take care of himself may wish to stay in the hospital so as not to be a burden on his family. Geriatric patients, particularly, feel that their care would be too burdensome for their aged spouses, children, or grandchildren. These elderly persons often have acute insight about the situation. Sometimes an aged parent believes that his effect upon the people with whom he lives is destructive. These geriatric patients choose nursing homes or hospitals as locales in which to end their trajectories; frequently this choice is also an acknowledgment of their low social loss to family life. (One highly emotional housewife in her 40's exclaimed that she would never be able to live in her house again if her aged father were to die there.) In contrast, younger adults who are dying worry less about their possible burden on wives and parents, for they sense that their social loss to family life is high, and that the family therefore will be more tolerant of the burden.

Fear of rejection by the persons the patient wants to have with him at death may also keep him from leaving the hospital. He may realize that a person about to die does not make very pleasant company, that the very imminence of death, as well as an intolerable or repugnant physical condition, may repulse even his intimate family. This fear distresses the dying patient, especially since his self-confidence is likely to be low; he may therefore prefer the impersonal isolation of the hospital staff to the risk of being isolated by the family he loves. Thus, an American patient, when wishing to go home to die among familiar circumstances and companions, thinks twice about what he has to offer, for his trajectory at this stage may well be unacceptable to others at home. In America, he knows, dying persons are typically avoided even by kinsmen. Dying among family at home becomes only a valued abstraction. So he chooses to die on a ward where his trajectory is acceptable and where he is sheltered from possible rebuffs by his family. In Europe and Asia, the home is still a more acceptable context for death.

If conditions do permit his dying at home—his condition is not too repugnant; the family wants him, will not avoid him, and will take the burden; his pain can be managed sufficiently well—the patient is likely to ask to die there. He will prefer this because dying at home gives him a greater chance to manage his own trajectory. If he gives orders to the hired nurse and family members caring for him, there is a greater probability that they will grant his wishes than that the hospital staff would. He is not in competition with other patients. He has a greater chance to control and negotiate his medicine and care in order to relieve pain more completely or to reduce prolonging. One patient kept asking to leave the hospital. Since she continually needed suctioning, the staff suspected that she wanted to die within hours at home—she was, in fact, trying to manage the end of her trajectory.

During the last hours of constant care, the patient is often especially sensitive about getting various attentions from the people around him. Hence, as he moves into this stage of his trajectory, it is particularly attractive to the patient to be at home, where he is not in competition with other patients. By contrast, during last hours in the hospital he must be screened off from other patients in order not to provide them with a disturbing death rehearsal. At home he is spared this isolation from friendly patients, which is enforced by hospital rules, yet he is provided with privacy.

In wishing to die at home, the patient typically focuses strongly on the companionship of the closest family member—parent, spouse, or child. In the stress of the last days and hours, he may not wish to see other kin or friends except for brief moments, but may desire the one intimate family member to be present constantly. The burden on this one member is much greater than on the other relatives or friends; he may be virtually trapped at the bedside until the patient's death. Amazingly enough, the dying patient often recognizes that the home setting is better able than the hospital both to permit this entrapment and to make it tolerable for his dear one.

In one case, an aging husband, all functions gone and inching toward death, wanted only his wife with him and no one else—no family, friends, or nurse. She ministered to his condition constantly and dared not leave him for more than fifteen minutes. The rest of the family wondered how she could endure it. The patient during his last hours was in no condition to worry about the burden he put on her; and the wife "stuck it out." In this way, when a hospital career is traded for a home career, the last days and hours may irreversibly trap a strong, intimate family member into managing the end of the trajectory. The entrapment can end only if the patient loses consciousness or dies quickly, or if the family member breaks down. . . .

THE MEANING OF DEATH

. . . [A] slow trajectory often gives the patient opportunities to come to terms with his own mortality, for his awareness and understanding may develop sufficiently early so that he can confront his dying. Such coming to terms involves two separate processes. The first consists of facing the annihilation of self, of visualizing a world without one's self. The second process consists of facing up to dying as a physical, and perhaps mental, disintegration. Some people are fearful of dying in great pain, or with extreme bodily disfiguration or with loss of speech, or are perhaps afraid of "just lying there like a vegetable." Some people think hardly at all about these aspects of dying, but tremble at the prospect of the disappearance of self. Moreover, some patients who have come to terms with the idea of death may only later focus on dying, especially when, as the trajectory advances, they are surprised, dismayed, or otherwise affected by bodily changes. On the other hand, someone who lives with his dying long enough may become assured that he will "pass" peacefully enough, and only then fully face the death issue.

These two issues, which generally loom large during the last sentient days, are certainly not unrelated; nor does coming to terms with them always constitute a final settlement. Unexpected turns in the trajectory are likely to unsettle previous preparations. With unexpected bodily deterioration, patients panic or begin to lose recognition of themselves as known identities. In one instance of great insight, a patient told a nurse she feared "comfort" surgery would cause her to "die twice." It might help to relieve her pain for a period, but eventually she would have to face dying again.

Most frequently, perhaps, patients come to terms by themselves or with the participation of close kin. Nurses, however, may be drawn into the processes. The patient typically initiates the "death talk"; the nurse tends to listen, to assent, to be sympathetic, to reassure. The nurse may even cry with a patient. Occasionally, a patient repeatedly invites nurses into conversations about death or dying, but they decline his invitations. Their refusals tend to initiate a drama of mutual pretense: neither party subsequently indicates recognition of the forthcoming death, although both know about it.

Other parties, too, sometimes play significant roles in these processes. In one such situation, an elderly patient was rescued from the isolation of mutual pretense by a hospital chaplain who directly participated in his coming to terms; eventually he also persuaded the wife, and to some extent the nurses, to enter into the continuing conversation. Patients sometimes rely on members of the clergy to move their spouses to faster acceptance of the inevitable and thus ease their own acceptance.

On the whole, American nurses seem to find it difficult to carry on conversations about death or dying with patients. Only if a patient has already come to terms with death, or if they can honestly assure him he will die "easily," if he is elderly, do they find it relatively easy to talk about such topics with him.[2] Unless a patient shows considerable composure about his dying, nurses and physicians lose their composure, except when they are specially trained or specially suited by temperament, or have some unusual empathy with a patient because of a similarity of personal history. When the patient's conversation during the last days is only obliquely about death and dying—consisting, for instance, of reminiscences of the past—and is not unpleasant or unduly repetitious, he has a better chance of inducing others, including the nurses, to participate in his closing of his life.

Clergymen also are expected, in most countries, to play major roles in this phasing-out of patients. A dying Greek patient who belonged to the Coptic faith completely upset the machinery of a Greek hospital by insisting late at night that he needed a Coptic priest immediately to give him his final communion. The request was almost impossible to fulfill at that hour, but the staff felt obliged to do so. A priest was found, but only just in time. In the United States, psychiatrists also sometimes perform analogous functions during the last phasing-out of more secularized patients.[3]

TYING UP LOOSE ENDS

An important aspect of a patient's coming to terms with impending death is the closing off of various aspects of everyday business. These include material and personal matters, like the drawing-up of wills and the making-up of quarrels. Physicians seem apt to allow businessmen to close off their business dealings, though a patient may have to insist on his right to do so, and to permit distraught families to urge reluctant patients to draw up, alter, or sign wills. A lawyer is sometimes brought in by the family or physician to help persuade the patient to make or alter his will. A chaplain or priest sometimes considers that his professional duties include bridging relationships between the dying person and an alienated spouse or offspring. One chaplain elatedly described how he had been instrumental in bringing a patient, her husband, her parents, and her children to face death together. This patient had gone ahead of her kinsmen in facing her death, and could no longer really talk with them. The chaplain bridged over the awkward relationships.

Sometimes the patient accepts his forthcoming death even before the staff has quite come to terms with it. Moreover, the patient's "social willing" may shock his family or the staff precisely because he has imaginatively reached his life's end before they have. One patient, for instance, relied on the intervention of his sister (who happened to be a nurse) to will his library to a neighboring college; his wife would never discuss the matter with him. A more extreme instance of social willing, which shocked personnel, was when a patient, during his last days, insisted on signing his own autopsy papers. This action struck the staff as singularly grotesque, despite the accepted similar practice of willing one's eyes, brain, or entire body to hospitals.

TEMPORAL INCONGRUITIES

Still another great barrier may block even the best-intentioned nurses and physicians from providing adequate help to a patient when he faces his demise: the immense difference between the staff's and the patient's conceptions of time. As we have noted repeatedly, the staff operates on "work time." Their tasks are guided by schedules, which on most wards are related to many patients, both dying and recovering. More important, and more subtle, work time with a given dying patient is a matter of timing work according to his expected trajectory. He is supposed to die more or less "on time," even when that time is uncertain. Our data, as well as accounts by dying patients or by kin who have participated intimately in relatives' dying, suggest that a patient's personal sense of time undergoes striking changes once he becomes aware of his impending death. This occurs whether he becomes aware very early or very late.

The last days become structured in highly personalized temporal terms. The future is foreshortened, cut out, or abstracted to "after I am gone." The personal past is likely to be reviewed and reconceptualized. The present takes on various kinds of personal meanings. Author Bernice Kavinovsky noted, for example: "All week, although I teach my classes, arrange for a substitute, put the dinner on, telephone my son at his apartment, shower, mark manuscripts, I perform each act almost clinically aware of the obstruction in my breast." She was "at the same time assailed on every hand by beauty's endless argument—an arc of light, or the curve of my husband's cheek . . . or the noise of the children's games on the roof next door"—the sights and sounds of the world taking on sudden and astonishing beauty.[4] Various semimystical experiences may be associated with the new temporal references. Things previously taken for granted are now savored as unique but unfortunately transitory. Occasional reprieves, recognized as only reprieves, evoke temporally significant reactions running from, "Oh, God! take me, I was prepared and now will not be prepared" to gratefulness for unexpected time.

The important point is not so much the variability of temporal reconstructions as the difficulty, and sometimes complete inability, of outsiders to grasp these personal reconstructions. One cannot know about them unless privy to the dying person's thoughts. He may keep them to himself, especially in a context of mutual pretense. He may not be able to express them clearly, especially when he becomes less sentient. A busy staff may have little time to listen or to invite revealing talk, particularly if patients are competing for attention. In many American hospitals nursing aides spend more time in patients' rooms than the nurses do, even during last days. When aides manage to grasp a patient's temporal reordering of his life, they may be unable to pass along this knowledge to the nurses, or not feel free to do so, or assume that the information is unimportant.

When the patient's personal time and the staff's work time are highly disparate, considerable strain may be engendered. Nor is the source of the trouble necessarily evident to either. Sometimes, of course, the staff does sense something of a patient's reconceptualizations, without necessarily realizing their deep import, and may somewhat adjust its own work time to his requirements. Thus on a medical ward housing many cancer patients, which we studied, there was a ward ideology of "letting them set the pace," with work time considerably structured around the patients' relatively slow tempo. Within limits, cancer patients could negotiate, for instance, to eat or have their temperatures taken later than when ordinarily scheduled. . . .

REFERENCES

1. Epilogue from *Ezio Pinza: An Autobiography* (New York: Rinehart, 1958), p. 278. Robert Magidoff co-authored this autobiography.
2. Jeanne C. Quint, *The Nurse and the Dying Patient* (New York: Macmillan, 1967); "Mastectomy—Symbol of Cure or Warning Sign?", *GP*, XXIX (March, 1964), pp. 119-24; "The Impact of Mastectomy," *The American Journal of Nursing,* 63 (November, 1963), pp. 88-92.
3. Personal communications from several psychiatrists.
4. *Voyage and Return: An Experience with Cancer* (New York: W. W. Norton, 1966), p. 20.

PART THREE

THE HEALTH CARE SYSTEM
AND CHRONIC ILLNESS

CHAPTER 15

PROVIDING BETTER CARE

"Now," the reader may well comment, "Parts One and Two of this book are quite illuminating: I have gotten both a general picture and many vivid illustrations of the problems of the chronically ill—but what about the practical side of all this? How can this information help a nurse, social worker, physical therapist, etc., like me, to provide better care to the patient?"

That is a perfectly legitimate question, but one must approach its answer with considerable caution. What we have in mind is that when anyone uses a phrase like "provide better care to the patient," rather than "how can we help these people," then one has already begun in a subtle way to lay professional claim to a domain which, perhaps, belongs more properly to the sick people and their families.

In the preceding pages, we have seen these people attempting, with more or less success and courage, to manage their lives, often in the face of extreme adversity. Their management is *their* business. Even when they get good aid and counsel from health personnel, they themselves ultimately bear the responsibility for facing *their* problems, making *their* adjustive arrangements, handling *their* social relations, and sometimes even taking the decision of whether to continue living or to die right out of the hands of the medical authorities, who ordinarily tend to keep life alive as long as it can be kept alive. Given the realities of this situation, health personnel may well ask: What then is our responsibility, really? For how much should or can we be responsible, and about what? Responsibility only inside the health facilities, or somewhat inside "their" homes, too?

Currently, health personnel tend to require that the patient delegate maximum responsibility to the staff whenever he enters a health facility, especially a hospital. The staff expects, and if necessary demands, that responsibility. The terrain is theirs and they have virtually complete autonomy over it. This is why some patients prefer to die at home, wishing to die as much as possible in their own ways rather than in a hospitalized style. "At home" they don't have to delegate or even share the responsibility for dying—or living while dying—with outsiders, no matter how medically skillful or well-meaning.

Health personnel observe this same dichotomy between home and health facility. In fact, it is notable that inside the facility they bear heavy burdens of responsibility for the patient's well-being and care. They may fight for his very life. They may become so concerned with his care and his health that they get "overinvolved." Rather frequently they appear, or actually become, brusque and unconcerned, pulling away from psychological investment in him so as not to become drained of emotion and energy. Ironically, when he leaves for "the outside" all will quickly tend to forget him, except his physician (if he has one, and many people do not). Forget him, that is, until he again enters the hospital or visits the clinic. Home is the patient's domain. The corollary: whatever happens to him there is essentially his own business, just as what happens to him at the health facility is believed to be mostly the personnel's business. That is a somewhat overdrawn picture of the home-facility dichotomy, but there is a great deal of truth to the picture.

That dichotomy made sense, perhaps, when disease was primarily of an infectious kind. The patient then was under medical care while in the hospital and sent home when pretty much out of danger. (In earlier periods, or with milder illnesses, he was perhaps treated at home entirely by an attending physician.) With the advent of widespread chronic disease, however, any sharp division between home and health facility would seem to be far too simple a solution to the problems faced by the chronically ill.

In light of these problems, a more rational approach is to soften the line between the two realms. Probably this would involve two major kinds of changes.

1. Sick people, when at the health facilities, would have a generally greater participation in the decisions made both about their care and its implementation.
2. The health care "system" would be extended in systematic ways so that health personnel could play more of a role in aiding sick people, and their families, to cope with problems attendant on chronicity.

Those changes involve at least a two-pronged attack. In Chapter 16 we shall approach these issues on the level of broad "public policy" considerations. Before doing that, however, we shall look at the issues from the standpoint of health personnel themselves. Since most are not now engaged in servicing patients at home but are working at various kinds of facilities, our discussion will pertain mainly to those facilities, and especially to those that I know best, namely hospitals and clinics.

•   •   •

Staff members certainly need to know more about the chronically ill who visit such facilities than they can have learned from reading Parts One and Two of this book. What they need additionally is rather *specific* information—either about individual patients or about types of patients who suffer from the particular diseases "seen" at the staff's work site. This information surely will not only be medical but will include the kinds of social and psychological data discussed in the foregoing pages. While many staff members are quite capable of getting such information, certain features of health facilities mitigate against the personnel's obtaining this information, sharing it, and acting effectively in terms of it.

"DOING" TASKS VERSUS UNDERSTANDING THE PERSON

Staff members are, first of all, focused on "doing"—that is, on carrying out their primary jobs. These inevitably are quite medical and procedural. To do these tasks requires the obtaining of information. One needs to know the kinds of physiological, biochemical, pharmacological, and procedural information that typically finds its way into the patient's medical record. This information, of course, is gathered by a variety of different personnel and by a variety of methods. But, we would emphasize, very little of it is of a social or psychological nature.

When it is, then either it tends to be fragmentary, and unsystematic by comparison with other types of recorded data, or it is gathered and reported because the patient is "difficult." If the latter, then the staff members may genuinely be attempting to discover why he is so, or they may understandably be giving vent to their feelings by reporting what they believe is true about him. Some personnel (especially nurses and social workers trained in schools which emphasize "interpersonal" aspects of care) may pay considerable attention to the psychological and social difficulties of patients. Often, however, they find themselves not getting much support from other personnel in this particular side of their work. Likewise, some personnel, such as the nursing aides in hospitals and clinics, may come to learn quite a bit about the personal lives of the patients, but they are not much called upon by their "superiors" or supervisors to report what they have learned. This kind of information is simply not much valued.

ACCOUNTABILITY AND NONACCOUNTABILITY

The chief reason for this general neglect of the experiential aspects of the chronically ill is that those aspects are regarded as quite peripheral to the responsibilities of the health personnel. By responsibilities, we mean not merely the staff's perceived task-oriented responsibilities, but its actual organizational and even legal ones. The staff is only genuinely *accountable* for getting and reporting certain types of information and for doing certain kinds of tasks.[3] The corollary is that it is *not* accountable, not organizationally responsible, for other kinds of information and other kinds of interaction with patients (and their kinsmen).

One can see this very clearly, for instance, with patients who have come to the hospital or clinic with pain related to a chronic disease. Even cursory inspection of medical-nursing records, or listening to reports from personnel to their superiors, makes it quickly evident that staff members are responsible only for communicating about certain actions and not about a great many others. Among the former actions, of course, are the giving and carrying out of orders about medication. There is also staff communication, though not necessarily required, concerning the problems of assessing his pain, about his "complaints" of pain, about certain other "problems" with him, and so on. The larger array of detail, however, pertaining to interaction with the patient, or what was learned about his biography or his experiential history with his disease and his pain, is reported only fortuitously. Everyone has done more, observed more, knows more, than he or she reports or talks about to colleagues and superiors. Certainly, they know much more than is put into the official records. What is true of patients in pain is equally true of patients who are dying from their chronic illnesses.

In connection with accountability and the flow of information among staff members, it is worth examining what happens when they meet up with an especially difficult or troublesome patient. Then the personnel are likely to talk over ways of "working with" him. Into the deliberations may enter much shrewdness and experience with similar patients. When this happens, what was essentially invisible action—actions by patients or personnel not reported back or observed by other personnel—becomes part of the staff's organized effort. This kind of temporary organization and accountability of effort can be termed ad hoc, because it arises around specific patients rather than being a permanent feature of the facility's organization.

In fact, so little does this ad hoc organization usually carry over to permanent organization that a rather peculiar situation develops at most health facilities. Each time that another difficult patient appears, the personnel will draw, either personally or collectively, on their experiences with similar patients encountered in the past. ("She's just like Mrs. Frisbee. Remember the problems we had with her? And how we managed her?") In that sense, there is a carryover of staff learning and experience. (It is often bitter experience and rather biased or ineffective "learning.") However, a neutral observer might note that there develops a rather amazing pattern of repeated interactional difficulties around particular kinds of patients—and wonder why the staff doesn't effectively work out sensible, permanent ways of either preventing or coping better with these recurrent difficulties.

The reason is that they are organizationally responsible for quite another order of events, namely, the carrying out of medical and medically supportive tasks. Behavior and interaction are important to personnel only insofar as they permit or hinder the carrying out of primary tasks. Hence, each person develops his or her own style of working with patients. That individualized style may be relatively unnoticed by other personnel (as with night nurses or staff who draw blood or position patients for x-rays). On the other hand, someone's style of working with patients may influence others, either because it seems effective or because the person has supervisory power. Nevertheless, such modes of handling patients are only infrequently raised to the level of self-conscious organizational approaches, based on a careful consideration of biographies and experiences of the types of patients most frequently seen by the staff. As for the patients' families, they are even less likely to be thought about in those considered terms.

The exceptions to this usual nonaccountability of the psychological and social aspects of medical or health care are most conspicuously found at special, and usually rather innovatively oriented, facilities whose staffs must deal with such matters as the problems of families of children dying of leukemia or with patients who have special kinds of diseases (such as kidney transplants). At such locales, the organizational effort is not necessarily effective, but at least it *is* organized. It is a genuine attempt to deal with repeated patterns of difficulty rather than merely to cope with the patterns on an ad hoc basis.

It is probable that until health personnel are genuinely responsible for the social and psychological aspects of giving care (as they are for the more purely medical and procedural aspects) there will be limited improvement in those aspects of care, except that which is effected fortuitously or temporarily because of an unusually skilled or compassionate or sensible staff member. Genuine accountability about the neglected aspects of care can be built into facilities only if their major authorities understand the crucial importance, for chronic care, of those aspects. Then they will convert that understanding into a commitment that will result in necessary changes in written and verbal communication systems. This kind of understanding and commitment is likely to come about only after considerable nationwide discussion, such as is now taking place about terminal care. That kind of discussion about chronic care seems only in its initial phases, although it is certainly beginning. Inevitably it must evolve, if only because of mounting concern among the citizens of most industrialized countries with the quality of life rather than with only standards of living or, as in less fortunate nations, with sheer individual physical survival.

Having read all that, our readers may feel discouraged by visions of the insignificance of their individual efforts. If one must wait for genuine organizational accountability, then what can be done all by oneself! The answer is: quite a bit.

THE PATIENT'S MULTIPLE BIOGRAPHIES

Undoubtedly, the place to begin is to recognize that health personnel, especially those who do not visit sick people at home, see them from a very peculiar angle of vision. They are apt to see only that portion of a patient's biography that pertains to their own work or that they learn during the course of doing their work with or around him. Distortion aside, and assuming they do learn true things about him, they are likely to grasp only a *small slice* of his total, relevant biography: relevant, that is, to giving him good health care.

One way of comprehending what is meant by a small slice of biography is simply to think back to the foregoing pages of this book wherein we considered the complexities of the chronic experience, even for people sick from comparatively mild or uncomplicated diseases. There is another way of comprehending the same point. Sick people have at least three different types of biography. First, they have had sequential (or chronological) experiences with their disease. Second, they have had biographical experiences with medical and health care—that is, with physicians and other health personnel ("legitimately medical" or not) and with various kinds of facilities. Third, they have had what may be termed a social biography, that is, a personal history of encounters with kinsmen, friends, acquaintances, work colleagues, and strangers.

The important question is, then, for any given patient or type of patient: which of these biographies does the caring personnel tend to overlook, and how much of it? Surely it would not be contentious to claim that rather little of the second biography and sometimes very little of the third biography are regarded as directly relevant by the personnel in the course of their various duties. Sometimes even the disease biography is little comprehended in its experiential aspect; that is, the staff comprehends very little of what the patient has lived through in terms of his symptoms and his regimens or even his medical crises.

Yet each of the three biographies can present major interactional problems— even affect the providing of good care—when the sick person visits a health facility. As a minor, but frequent, instance consider the psychological and physiological difficulties of someone who has been accustomed to taking pain medications of a certain kind, a certain strength, and at certain intervals of time. He comes to the hospital where the staff takes over the work of giving him relief from his pain and, without consulting him, changes one or more of those variables. Patients sometimes warn nurses and attending physicians about specific drugs that they know from experience will be ineffective as pain killers or trigger allergic reactions, only to have warnings ignored, at cost to themselves. In general, nursing and medical personnel get to know little or nothing about a patient's past experience with pain—including his methods of dealing with it, other than the present or current evolving pain.[2] That is, they understand little of his experiential or management biography with regard to this kind of symptom.

Patients with severe chronic back pain, for instance, often come into hospitals for operations, hopeful that "this one" may accomplish what one or more other operations did not, but, at the same time, highly mistrustful of health personnel who previously have misdiagnosed, misoperated, mismanaged, or just plain scoffed at their "complaints." So they often prove to be difficult patients.[4] As for those with considerable experiences in hospitals, they can cause plenty of bad feeling when they make nasty comparisons between the handling of the medications here and there or comment pointedly about what they think is the incompetent production of unnecessary pain, as when certain procedures or tests are done on them. To continue with examples from pain: Back pain patients are frequently regarded by kinsmen and friends as, at least, somewhat hypochrondriacal, as not having "that much" pain. By not grasping the sick person's own understanding of his pain and of his experiences with others' definitions of it, health personnel are failing to give themselves the basis for providing more adequate care. Indeed, they are likely, by dubbing him neurotic or "a complainer," simply to be adding to his unfortunate social and medical care biographies.

So the very first place to begin improving the care of the chronically ill is to develop effective methods for discovering their actual biographies. That is true for each patient. It is also true for patients who suffer from the most typical diseases encountered at given locales. Surely, the next step is to utilize this information. While its fullest utilization cannot take place until there is an organized accountability for its collection and use, is there any question that considerable improvement of care can occur even without systematic accountability?

INTERVIEWING FOR BIOGRAPHICAL DATA

How, then, does one obtain this biographical information? Clearly, the first requisite is an attitude: "this information can be useful." If one believes otherwise, the effort to obtain the information will not be long extended—and it will be all too easy to slip back into disregarding or misconstruing whatever information has been discovered. Given a belief in the crucial importance of biographical data, however, it is still necessary to learn or develop effective methods for getting those data.

A social scientist would tend to say that the methods already exist. They need only be adjusted to the specific situations obtaining at any given health locale. What he would mean is that personnel could learn or be taught to use interviewing and observational techniques where they do not now really use them, or to use them more skillfully than they do now. A brief list of possibly useful books and articles about such techniques is given in the Bibliography. Short of exhorting readers to peruse them—and to urge supervisors to institute in-service courses on interviewing and observation—what specific instruction can be given here?

INTERVIEWING WHILE WORKING: "ACTION INTERVIEWS"

Let us look at interviewing, which is the chief instrumentality for getting biographical data. Seemingly, interviewing takes a great deal of time, and time often or usually is a scarce commodity for personnel. By contrast, social science researchers are paid or have proper incentives to spend all the time required to get good interview information; but personnel are not paid for that kind of work! A researcher may be able to spend 1, 2, 3, or more hours with "an interviewee," thus getting the requisite information. What health worker can work at that leisurely, talkative pace?

Wasted time or time given to other priorities aside, the issue of time is very germane. Yet, there are certain advantages that can accrue to a health worker that even a researcher does not always, or indeed usually, have. The basic fact about the patient–health worker relationship is that it is a service relationship. So the personnel are repeatedly doing something for, or at least around, the sick person. Thus most interviews—that is, conversations designed to get information—will be "action interviews." The conversations will take place while the staff member is in action—working. Of course, sometimes the patient (or kinsman) and staff member can just be chatting or spending relatively free time together, but most often they meet only when something is to be done to or for the patient.

Interviewing while working has its disadvantages, of course, but it can also have great advantages. To begin with, often the talk can go on while the work is proceeding. The staff member may initiate the talk or the particular topics, but so may the sick person. It is easier for some people (both patient and staff) to talk, in fact, about certain topics under such work conditions. One does not have to look directly into the other's face. One can take cues about what to say or ask from the very action itself. One can choose this time and place to say something, precisely because he does not expect the conversation to go on—or deeper. One can tentatively introduce a topic—as patients do—to see whether the staff member will pick up the conversational invitation, or turn away, or "turn the conversation off." (A skillful or determined staff member can do that with patients, too.)

Moreover, these action interviews usually need not be confined to a single session. A staff member is very likely to work with, or around, a patient repeatedly (although the intervals between sessions are shorter in hospitals than in clinics). Consequently, not all the information-getting need be jammed into a single encounter. Indeed, the very nature of "repeated sessions" means that the conversations are likely to be relatively short. But the next conversations can continue where preceding ones broke. That is, the total conversation is a continuing one, even though it may not be carried on whenever the two people meet. Repeated meetings also mean that each can more easily choose when and when not to talk. Thus a patient who seems not inclined to talk today, or this morning, need not be pushed to talk. One waits for a more appropriate mood.

Furthermore, continuing conversations yield at least two other potential advantages. As the interviewer learns more and more, he or she will find that this cumulative knowledge will enable better questions to be asked. (By questions, we do not necessarily mean direct questions posed to the patient, but kinds of information about which the staff member will seek information.) Thus the information obtained is not only quantitatively cumulative but has a tendency to become qualitatively better. Besides that, continuing interviews tend to go "deeper," because both parties feel increasingly free to express themselves. Especially is this true of many patients in health settings. The reasons are several but include previous bad experiences with health workers or mistrust of health personnel in general. Some patients do not feel free to talk about themselves in a setting so different from their own home. Some just take time to reveal themselves. And, of course, most people need to test out listeners before going deeper into what matters to their private selves. Will the listener really listen? Understand? Pass a bad judgment? Be sympathetic? Naturally, the more a staff member reveals of himself or herself—if only that he is sympathetic, empathetic, compassionate, or has had similar personal experiences—the deeper this continuing conversation can go.

INTERVIEWS ARE CONVERSATIONS

That is all very well, the reader of this book may say, but how can a person who is not specially trained in interviews do this kind of interviewing? A partial answer to that query is that, perhaps, too much of a mystique has been built around the idea of the skilled interviewer. We would not for a moment assert that training is unnecessary, or that some people can be taught to be skillful at interviewing while others are pretty hopeless. However, in our opinion, it makes eminent sense to think of interviews quite as if they were conversations. An interview is different only insofar as its special purpose is to get information from the talk that flows between the conversationalists. If the conversation does not yield good information, then it may be good talk but a poor interview. Talk and conversation it is, however, and not much more.

Now, the fact that every interview is supposed to yield information has important implications for health personnel. Possibly the foremost is that they need not be especially frightened of, or anxious about, the *idea* of interviewing. All of us attempt to get information from certain of the conversations in which we engage our friends, relatives, strangers, officials. Some of us are better at getting that information than are others. But all of us can get some information—especially if it matters!

Another implication of the idea of interview-as-conversation is that all of us are better at some conversations than at others. Some people can talk more freely with intimates than with strangers; some, just the reverse. (Example: some persons can talk easily with strangers in the park; others find it nearly impossible to strike up or even engage in such conversations.) Some can talk better on the run, or while doing something, than when self-consciously face to face with someone. Some people are marvelously good listeners, so by their very presence and posture they invite others to confide private detail to them; while others are very good at getting people to express themselves by dint of aggressive questioning or lively verbal interplay.

In consequence, everybody (including every research interviewer) is better at some kinds of conversations than at others. He can neither be equally good at all of them nor hope to learn to be very competent at every variety. The most that can be hoped is that he can discover, be aware of, what his genuine limitations are. It is precisely at the margins of conversational competence where people need special training. They need to learn what they think, or feel, they cannot do—or cannot do very well. Then they need to stretch themselves to discover whether, in fact, that is really where their limits are; or whether they need to "push themselves," or perhaps to get special encouragement or a few specific techniques in order to get over some temperamental or experiential barrier.

It seems safe to say that it is far more important that interviewers learn the limits of their natural repertoire, and learn how to extend those limits, than that they learn very specific techniques. Certainly techniques are useful: the problem, however, is that they apply only to certain kinds of conversations (interviews) and not necessarily to others. Advice not to interrupt the other's flow of talk is certainly useful for success at certain kinds of interviews but scarcely applies to interviews that involve putting the informant under great pressure, as with captured spies or suspected criminals. Similarly, the techniques used especially by psychiatrists, or derived from their teachings, are not necessarily going to work effectively with patients who are asking explicitly for information—and thus yielding information about themselves to an astute interviewer, who needs to be answering to interviewees as they are requesting rather than in terms of his conception that they need therapeutic handling.

These last examples allow us to raise another useful issue about interviewing. Information obtained from conversations is valid only to the extent that one can make good judgments about what the conversation was really all about. To take an obvious example: if the interviewee is deliberately faking, putting one off the scent, then his falsified story simply ought not to be believed. But one cannot make that judgment unless one knows, or suspects, that falsification actually transpired. From the very nature of the conversation what really transpired is not necessarily an easy thing to determine, though obviously we can be far more certain about some conversations than others. At any rate, the injunction to the interviewer is to discover with as much probability as possible what kind of identity the other person assigned both to "himself" and to "me" during the conversation. Who was I to him, as he saw it, and what was he explicitly or implicitly trying to be to me? (This matter of estimating the situational identities of interviewee and interviewer is so important that one must wonder about even social science research, based on interviews or questionnaires, if the research does not make clear what those juxtaposed identities were.) What will help the health worker in making those kinds of estimates is precisely that the interviews, characteristically, are repeated, continuous, and based generally on a service relationship. For all that, health personnel will need to develop to the utmost their sensitivities about the identity aspects of their interview-conversations.

MULTIPLE INTERVIEWS

Finally, a word about another advantage that personnel may enjoy in their interviewing. Chronic illness, as we have repeatedly said, usually involves the kinsmen as well as the sick person himself. Consequently, when kinsmen show up at the facility, some ought to be interviewed also. Naturally, there will be discrepancies among their views and between each of them and the patient himself. That difficulty should not persuade any staff member from his duty of having, somehow, the responsibility of putting together as accurate a story as is possible. In fact, the very existence of discrepancies sometimes is not so much a deterrent to discovering the truth as an aid in discovering how the different people in the family see what has happened both to the sick person and to the family relationships. That is immensely important information for the health personnel to have if—in accordance with the viewpoint of this book—they are to give better care to the patient himself.

Moreover, health personnel have the special advantage often of being in the position of talking not merely with each family member separately but with two or more (including the patient) together. Naturally, there are also disadvantages to these multiple person interviews. This type of interview situation can also yield very useful information. People will say certain things—and in certain ways—in this context that they might not when alone with an interviewer.

PATIENTS WILL TALK!

Before leaving the topic of interviewing for biographical data, we should make *the* most important point: the chronically ill (and their families) usually are more than willing to give those data. Many sick persons, as we have noted earlier, are not able to tell other people about their difficulties, or refrain from doing so for a variety of reasons, and some suffer from genuine social isolation. The researchers who interviewed the sick persons whose problems are described in Part Two discovered how eager most of them were to talk about themselves and their disease-related problems. (To quote from an apt speech by Mr. Doolittle in G. B. Shaw's *Pygmalion*: "I'm willing to tell you, I'm *wanting* to tell you. . . .") Health personnel who are genuinely interested in the chronically ill should have no less success in engaging them in informational conversations. While the researchers had more time, and perhaps greater interviewing skill, health personnel have the great advantage of direct access and a service relationship to the sick persons.

USES OF BIOGRAPHICAL INFORMATION

The next question is: after the biographical information is obtained, what does one do with it? The answer is: use it! Any innovative person can surely figure out how to do so. In general, however, there are three ways to use the information. The first, and most obvious, is that any individual staff member will shape his or her own responses to the sick person in accordance with what is known about him so that, presumably, more individualized care can be given. It may even be possible to persuade other staff members that one's information helps to give a fuller picture of a patient's current state. If so, more than one staff member will act on that information. Staff discussion, even when debate then ensues, should lead to more considered action toward the patient than if no interview had been reported.

More important than improving care for specific patients, however, is what interviews can do for the care of patients in general. What we have in mind is that every facility and every subpart of the facility draws patients who have certain kinds of illness. Whether that means this particular clinic gets arthritic clients while another gets asthmatic ones, or whether the latter clinic draws both elderly and adolescent asthmatic patients—in either case, the disease-related experiences of their respective clients will vary. The implication is that interviewing should be focused not merely on individual patients but on patterns of patients. Once a staff begins to obtain this more extensive—and deeper—knowledge of the biographies of "our types" of patients, then interviews with specific patients and families will be easier to carry out and be far more revealing. If staff members do not feel confident to do this kind of interviewing, then it may be sensible to attempt to persuade the administration to hire a researcher who can help get that information. However, many staffs could get the data once they believed in their usefulness or, as we would claim, in their necessity. In any event, the road to genuine accountability, to organizational responsibility, lies in the direction of discovering these more general biographical patterns and then in a concerted effort to respond to them.

SHARED RESPONSIBILITY

Getting and interpreting biographical data brings us squarely up against the next important and indeed crucial question. How much responsibility for his care should be left to the patient when he is at the health facility? As noted earlier, he has almost total responsibility when at home, but what about "here"? In general, the answer to the question is that once staff members really begin to respect the patient's biographies (medical, medical care, and social), then they will listen more closely to what he thinks good care must include for himself. We need not always take his views "straight," but most of the time they should be taken into account. Again, innovative personnel should be able to determine the limits of a given patient's responsibility for aspects of care when at the facility. They will thereby not only save themselves much trouble with so-called difficult patients but greatly contribute to the betterment of care. Most important, perhaps, they will give the patient that much additional support for dealing with his symptoms, regimens, disease, and people in the outside world. Also, they may even elect to organize the facility's work in somewhat different or at least additional ways.

REFERENCES

1. Schatzman, Leonard, and Strauss, Anselm: Field research: strategies for a natural sociology, Englewood Cliffs, New Jersey, 1973, Prentice-Hall, Inc.
2. Strauss, Anselm, Fagerhaugh, Shizuko, and Glaser, Barney: Pain: an organizational-work-interactional perspective, Nursing Outlook 22:560-566, 1974.
3. Strauss, Anselm, Glaser, Barney, and Quint, Jeanne: The non-accountability of terminal care, Hospitals 38:73-87, 1964.
4. Wiener, Carolyn: Pain assessment, pain legitimation and the conflict of staff-patient perspectives, Nursing Outlook, 1975.

CHAPTER 16

PUBLIC POLICY AND CHRONIC ILLNESS

Beyond the responsibility and, indeed, the power of individuals who work as health personnel is the task of changing the present societal status of the chronically ill. Nevertheless, there surely is a place in this book for at least a brief discussion of general policy considerations. Some health workers could play a role, and others now are certainly doing so, in getting policy changes effected.

The larger public is aware, of course, of the special difficulties of being sick when old or poor, and a few well-publicized diseases have their interested and involved publics. Yet the chronically ill, as such, are not defined, at least in the United States, as what sociologists call "a social problem" (poverty or pollution or the American racial problem). Perhaps chronic illness should not be defined as a social problem. Nevertheless, a more general awareness should be fostered of how society is arranged, physically, socially, and financially, for normal people and of what this means for sick people. Doubtless, the efforts of specific interest groups would be rendered more effective if such an across-the-board awareness were to develop. Currently the approaches tend to be categorically oriented, that is, focused on specific diseases or types of disease (heart, cancer). If the chronically ill are to be aided in their own efforts to live more effectively and happily, the categorical approaches simply will not get them very far. That is, after all, one of the chief messages of this book.

NEGLECTING THE MOBILITY NEEDS OF ILL PERSONS

A telling way of underlining how disregarded, or at least unnoticed, are the needs of the chronically ill is to consider briefly how American streets and public buildings are ordinarily organized, then to raise questions about that in terms of sick people who have persistent mobility problems because of lack of energy or physical disablement. On the downtown streets of most towns and cities are there many (or any) benches—including at the bus stops? Are the curbstones set low enough to make them manageable or are they troublesome and difficult? Are the entrances to public buildings (including the hospitals and clinics) led up to by ramps or steps? Are they with or without railings? Are the entry doors easy to manage or do they require great expenditure of energy to open? Is seating at theaters—and churches—arranged for normal people or are some seats, at least, arranged for people with mobility difficulties? That list of questions could easily be extended, and to each there is usually a negative answer.

That the standard terrain can be so difficult is realized by normal people only when they are temporarily incapacitated in limb or energy. Ordinarily, they are no more aware of such a list of obstacles than of how a similar terrain might look to a cat or a giraffe. To prove this point to themselves, health personnel might have a look at the entries and entrance doors to their own facilities, also at the floors of their lobbies and corridors (polished and shining or carefully carpeted?).

The mobility difficulties of the chronically ill when in public places provides a clear exemplification of a crucially important issue. Not only is chronicity much more than a medical problem, it is one, also, in which the public, whether with recognition or not, is deeply implicated. Of course, one cannot fault public authorities, or private builders either, for aggravating the physical difficulties of the ill, since they do not realize their own contributions in that matter. Indeed, there exist specialized books and articles written by disabled persons for disabled persons that give information about how to get in and around in specific public places and buildings. While these writings are of help to their readers, they ordinarily do not reach public officials or carry an accusatory argument to the general public. By the same token, however, only a public awareness and an arousal of conscience about these issues will ease the mobility difficulties of sick people when in public places.

A GENERAL STRATEGY

All this suggests a general strategy for attacking the question of the division of labor among those who might be responsible for better management of the problems attendant on chronic illness. In the first place, the sick person *and* his agents are much concerned with handling those problems. For health personnel, or anyone else, to attempt to usurp their responsibilities would be ultimately ineffective, and also quite possibly immoral in implications. On the other hand, it is in the public interest, and perhaps eventually will impinge on the public's conscience, that normal arrangements should take into account at least some of the problems of the chronically ill. Questions of cost are involved, of course, but as the mobility illustration implies, cost may be far less consequential than simple lack of awareness.

Beyond the general public or special interest publics, we might consider health personnel themselves, along with the occupations, professions, and institutions they represent. What overall role should they play? The answer, perhaps, is twofold. On occasion, they can act as members of interested publics with respect to specific issues. Generally, however, they should be concerned with extending the so-called health care system (such as it is in the United States), extending it, that is, so as to aid the sick and their families much more than at present.

NEED FOR A WIDER RANGE OF SERVICES

Since that is only the most sweeping of positions, what about more specific policy suggestions? Here, the very pertinent suggestions of Laura Reif can be quoted[1]:

> A wider range of services [for the chronically ill] is imperative. . . . The numbers and types which could be utilized . . . are legion. . . . The following broad categories of help are relevant:
>
> *Broad-spectrum counseling and education* addressed to the sick person *and* his associates: counseling on both the medical and social-psychological aspects of managing a chronic illness (i.e., help in tailoring regimes so they entail fewer costs and obtain greater benefits for overall functioning; assistance in developing social skills in dealing with visible disability, stigma, social isolation; managing the impact of illness on others; renegotiating responsibilities with family and employers, taking account of the constraints of illness; help managing the social, personal, and medical aspects of terminal disease; legal counsel regarding the ramifications of diagnosis and treatment—as help dealing with employer discrimination, termination of insurance coverage, and loss of license due to illness).
>
> Assistance in *revamping the physical environment,* taking into account the limitations resulting from illness and disability (i.e., designing or modifying living accommodations, work areas, transportation facilities in order to improve the physical settings in which the chronically ill live and work).
>
> Assistance with *funding* and *money-management:* providing financial resources, budget-planning, and other economic-management help to the sick person and those affected by the economic ramifications of his chronic illness (this involves extension of economic assistance to cover not only the medically-related but the social and personal "costs" of chronic illness—i.e., the expense of revamping work areas, the cost of equipment to facilitate functioning, reimbursing lost pay, etc.).
>
> *Redesigning social arrangements:* organization of individual and group effort in the interest of providing the necessary man-power for dealing with the ramifications of chronic illness (i.e., working with the sick person and his associated others, or with groups of chronically ill in the interest of providing emergency back-up systems, task exchange networks, or social support arrangements—for the purpose of sustaining persons who must regularly deal with the ramifications of chronic illness).
>
> *Supplying technical aid and equipment:* designing and providing new equipment and techniques to facilitate daily activities for those who have disabilities, and for those who care for the chronically ill (i.e., such equipment might be designed to facilitate regime procedures, household tasks, mobility, etc.).
>
> *Medical intervention:* provision of broad-spectrum medical services, including use of paramedical resources such as dietary counseling, rehabilitation services, speech therapy, services of voluntary groups—these efforts directed toward improving the overall functioning of the individual, *taking into account* the potential existence of multiple diseases, co-existing disabilities, and the resulting personal and social ramifications of illness.
>
> *Daily-maintenance services:* supplying assistance with various aspects of daily living—household tasks, personal care, chauffeur and other travel services, and so forth.

Public education and *informational services:* These would be the counterpart of counseling of the sick person—they involve educating those persons who are likely to encounter or care for the chronically ill; they also involve attempts to increase understanding, lessen misconceptions, and limit prejudicial behavior on the part of those who are likely to affect the lives and opportunities of the chronically ill and disabled.

Managerial assistance: making available to clients an agent (whether brokers, contractors-of-services, ombudsmen, or advocates) who could insure access to, and effective provision of, services to the sick person and his involved associates. Such client-representatives could provide assistance in the following sorts of areas: (1) obtaining information and services; (2) assisting clients in decision-making re use of services; (3) coordinating specialized services; (4) insuring quality care; and/or (5) facilitating feed-back from consumers, with respect to existing and needed services.

Mrs. Reif goes on to say that these:

. . . potentially effective resources are much broader in scope than those presently utilized. Because current services tend to revolve around medically-pertinent interventions, the resources most frequently utilized tend to be medical and paramedical. There is no reason to believe that many—if not the majority—of services . . . need to be supplied by medically-trained personnel, or provided through specifically medical institutions.

The providers of such services could include unions, commercial and industrial organizations, lay self-help groups, the mass media, and agencies both private and governmental.

Since the actual or potential unemployment of the chronically ill is an important problem for them and their families, a substantial public effort needs to be directed at protecting their rights to work. This means getting the appropriate legislation passed and enforced by governmental agencies or the courts. Mrs. Reif also suggests employer education regarding the work potential of various groups of the chronically ill, tax incentives for employers who retain or hire the chronically ill worker, and union support against companies for members who are unjustifiably denied employment. Thus in the matter of employment, as in other areas, there probably will be need for informational campaigns, private (and consumer) action, and also a certain amount of governmental action, in order to protect what hopefully will be defined as the rights of chronically ill citizens.

NEEDED: A MORE RESPONSIVE HEALTH INDUSTRY
Redesigning current health facilities

Finally, what about the host of personnel who are involved in what is sometimes called the health care industry? Basically, the two main issues here are as follows: First of all, as emphasized previously, within health facilities personnel should work toward establishing accountability for the behavioral and interactional aspects of chronic care, along with giving the sick person more "say" in his care when within the facility. In addition, the organization of the facilities needs to be redesigned so that the chronically ill can better use their services.

As many observers have noted, clinics and medical centers are often awkwardly located and their services are inconveniently scheduled for many of their potential clients. Chronically ill people, low in energy, with mobility problems and difficult regimen schedules and the like, are often hard put to get to certain facilities and at the institutionally scheduled times. Moreover, the sources of information that they or any other sick person—but especially they—need about available services are far from adequate. Generally the facilities

> . . . have not considered the larger problem of making their services known. . . . Little has been done to locate those who want or need help in dealing with chronic disease and its ramifications.[1]

Those who do get to the facility often fail to gain entry—they cannot handle the admission procedures, cannot adequately verbalize or justify their need for aid, leave treatment programs because they lack time or energy or sufficient help in finding their way around the health system, and so on. "What [they] need most is help in routing themselves through the organizational network [of facilities] and into the kinds of services they can most effectively utilize."[1] Moreover, although the selection of clients by facilities understandably functions to get the desired match between services and clients, the selection procedures do leave many sick persons with no ready access to health services.

Extending the facilities

The second direction in which the health care system must go is toward proferring far more and additional kinds of counsel and aid to the chronically ill and their families. This would require building a more general recognition of the range of management problems attendant on suffering from various chronic conditions. It means the training and education of health personnel in these matters. Presumably, new categories of personnel (health or health-related) would also be needed including health consumer advocates, social-psychological counselors, and coordinators of various health and health-related services. Again, we turn to the adjective "innovative" to suggest that brains combined with practical experience would allow health personnel to invent new modes of offering services (and to fill gaps between current servicing agencies). The kind of extended and comprehensive medical/health program needed for many chronically sick persons is exactly what they rarely get today. If they are so unfortunate as to suffer from two or more diseases, those deficiencies of service are even more pronounced.

A last few words

Beyond that, it is necessary to emphasize again that helping sick people to live more satisfying lives is not only, or even principally, the responsibility of health personnel. If the many kinds of services listed earlier are to be offered to the ill and their families, then many other interested participants must enter into what now looks like the "health" arena. Among the participants in this era of consumer movements will surely be ill persons themselves as well as their legislative and legal agents—also additional types of agents who will voluntarily or on a paid basis take up their cause. Health personnel should be only too pleased, or perhaps relieved, not to have to shoulder the entire burden of work. Part of the aim of this book has been to suggest how they can *offer* better service to the chronically ill. Remember, it is the *chronically* ill who constitute the bulk of the sick population in "advanced" nations.

REFERENCE

1. Reif, Laura: A policy perspective and its implications, unpublished paper. Department of Social and Behavioral Science, School of Nursing, University of California, San Francisco.

EPILOGUE

Just as this book was nearing completion, I happened to read Joshua Horn's *Away With All Pests*,[1] a moving account of what Horn, a British physician, saw in China from 1954 to 1969 while working as a surgeon, teacher, and medical field worker. One incident that he recounts, although not about chronic disease as such, is so relevant to our own inquiry that I cannot refrain from commenting on it.

Horn begins the incident by saying that the concept of full responsibility had taken on a deeper meaning after coming to China. "Although in the past I always thought of myself as being responsible, it is becoming clear that to be fully responsible requires more than good intentions." Horn then tells about a middle-aged peasant on whom he had operated. Terribly burned in a home accident, the man was rushed to the hospital where emergency treatment temporarily saved him. "At this point we paused to consider the problem as a whole"—"we" being the surgeons. "Some of the doctors thought it was impossible to save his life and doubted whether we should fruitlessly prolong his agony." But the two villagers who had rushed the unfortunate man to the hospital urged attempts to save him. "They explained that he was chairman of the Association of Former Poor Peasants in his Commune, that everybody respected him for his unselfish service and would look after him very well."

So the physicians resolved to do everything possible. However, two opposing views of how to proceed then developed: should amputation of his legs be delayed until his condition had improved sufficiently to get him through the formidable operation, or was a delay even more dangerous? "Gradually, through argument, it became clear that these opposing viewpoints did not result from different estimations of the medical aspects of the case but, in essence reflected two different attitudes toward responsibility and taking risks." No surgeon, Horn says, wants the risk of a patient's death on the operating table; it is distressing and "harmful to his reputation." So, "concern for one's reputation and peace of mind may, even though unconsciously, influence a surgeon's decisions." However, they began to realize the nonmedical bases of their potential decision, and "determined to be guided by Mao's insistence on a full sense of responsibility"

151

(that is, communal responsibility), they then finally reached agreement upon doing the kind of operation—and doing it immediately—that perhaps might be successful. (It was.)

What lessons can one draw from this story? After all, China is a communist society and not an "advanced" industrialized, urbanized nation like the United States. We don't have communes, or even the kinds of village communities that take total and personal responsibility for caring for a permanently incapacitated man; nor do surgeons so respect the head of state as to follow his perspective on responsibility in guiding their professional ethics and procedures. Nevertheless, Horn's narrative does underscore what might be striven for and possibly attained in countries like ours—but of course in our own political and social styles.

I have in mind that the implications of Horn's incident include the following.

1. That there can be a much more explicit and better balanced division of labor between health personnel and the rest of the population. The latter should have much more responsibility for decision-making and more explicit functions in caring for the sick.

2. Yet health personnel should be appreciated (provided they earn the appreciation) for their skills, judgment, and trained wisdom.

3. Health personnel should also be regarded, and regard themselves, as acting in the service of their clients—not dominate them, especially in the health facilities, or make decisions for them (indeed often decisions unknown to them).

4. They should listen closely to the sick persons and their representatives and not impose their own viewpoints—which at best will be unheeded (away from the health facilities) and at worst can be disastrous.

5. In short, for the best care, there need to be *intelligent transactions* carried out among sick persons, their representatives, and health personnel.

Horn's village peasant was not a "patient," a "case," a "client"—he was a fellow citizen. He was brought to the hospital for traumatic emergency care. Chronic disease necessitates even more urgent attention to what Horn refers to as a deeper sense of responsibility. The challenge, presumably, is whether this can be achieved in noncommunist countries as well as the Chinese seem to have met the challenge. Whether communist China has been able to institute this kind of civic responsibility as well as Horn claims is not the point; rather, can this be achieved in other countries, including the United States, each in its own style? Yes? No? Maybe?

REFERENCE

1. Horn, Joshua: Away with all pests, New York, 1969, Monthly Review Press.

BIBLIOGRAPHY

BIOGRAPHY AND AUTOBIOGRAPHY

Campanella, Roy: It's good to be alive, New York, 1959, Dell Publishing Co., Inc.

Gunther, John: Death be not proud, New York, 1949, Harper & Row, Publishers.

Hodgins, E.: Episode: report on the accident inside my skull, New York, 1964, Atheneum Publishers.

Lowenstein, Prince Leopold of: A time to love . . . a time to die, New York, 1971, Doubleday & Co., Inc.

Kaehele, Edna: Living with cancer, New York, 1952, Doubleday & Co., Inc.

Kavinovsky, Bernice: Voyage and return: an experience with cancer, New York, 1966, W. W. Norton & Co., Inc.

Kesten, Yehuda: Diary of a heart patient, New York, 1968, McGraw-Hill Book Co.

Massie, Robert: Nicholas and Alexandra, New York, 1967, The Bobbs-Merrill Co., Inc. See especially pp. 147-164 ("A Mother's Agony").

McIvers, Patricia: Good night, Mr. Christopher, New York, 1974, Sheed and Ward, Inc.

Ritchie, Douglas: Stroke: a diary of a recovery, London, 1960, Faber & Faber, Ltd.

Wertenbaker, Lael: Death of a man, New York, 1957, Random House, Inc.

RESEARCH AND PROFESSIONAL

Benoliel, Jeanne Quint: Becoming diabetic, Ph.D. thesis, School of Nursing, University of California, San Francisco, 1969.

Benoliel, Jeanne Quint: The developing diabetic identity. In Batey, M.: Communicating nursing research, Boulder, Colorado, 1970, Wiche.

Calkins, Kathy: Shouldering a burden, Omega 3:23-36, 1972.

Charmaz, Kathy C.: Time and identity: the shaping of selves of the chronically ill, Ph.D. thesis, University of California, San Francisco, 1973.

Chronic conditions and limitations of activity and mobility, U. S., July 1965-June 1967, Public Health Service Publication No. 1000, Series 10-#61, U.S. Department of Health, Education, and Welfare, Public Health Services, Mental Health Administration, January, 1971.

Chu, George: The kidney patient: a socio-medical study, Ph.D. thesis, School of Public Health, University of California, Berkeley, 1975.

Cogswell, B., and Weir, W.: A role in process: development of medical professionals' role in long-term care of chronically diseased patients, Journal of Health and Human Behavior 5:95-106, 1973.

Dana, Bess: The integration of medicine with other community services. In Catastrophic illness: impact on families, challenge to the professions, New York, 1966, Cancer Care, Inc., National Cancer Foundation.

Danowski, T., editor: Diabetes mellitus, New York, 1964, American Diabetic Association.

Davis, Fred: Passage through crisis: polio victims and their families, Indianapolis, 1963, The Bobbs-Merrill Co., Inc.

Davis, Fred: Deviance disavowal: the management of strained interaction by the visibly handicapped, Social Problems 9:121-132, 1961. Also reprinted in Davis, Fred: Illness, interaction and the self, Belmont, California, 1972, Wadsworth Publishing Co.

Davis, Marcella: Living with multiple sclerosis, Springfield, Illinois, 1973, Charles C Thomas, Publisher.

Dubuskey, M., editor: The chronically ill child and his family, Springfield, Illinois, 1970, Charles C Thomas, Publisher.

Fagerhaugh, Shizuko: Mismatched properties: problems in managing mentally ill TB patients, Ph.D. thesis, School of Nursing, University of California, San Francisco, 1972.

Fagerhaugh, Shizuko, and Frankel, H.: Behind the scenes, the skid row hotel manager who sees that Ernie takes his TB drugs, The Bulletin, National TB Respiratory Disease Association, vol. 56, 1970.

Futterman, E., and Hoffman, I.: Crisis and adaptation in the families of fatally ill children. In Anthony, E., and Koupernik, C.: The child in his family: the impact of disease and death, New York, 1973, John Wiley and Sons, Inc., pp. 127-143.

Futterman, E., Hoffman, I., and Sabshin, M.: Parental anticipatory mourning. In Kutscher, A., editor: Psychosocial aspects of terminal care, New York, 1972, Columbia University Press, pp. 243-272.

Glaser, Barney, and Strauss, Anselm: Awareness of dying, Chicago, 1965, Aldine Publishing Co.

Glaser, Barney, and Strauss, Anselm: Time for dying, Chicago, 1967, Aldine Publishing Co.

Goffman, Erving: Stigma: notes on the management of spoiled identity, Englewood Cliffs, New Jersey, 1963, Prentice-Hall, Inc.

Griffith, C.: Sexuality and the cardiac patient, Heart and Lung 2:70-73, 1973.

Gussow, Z.: Behavioral research in chronic disease: a study of leprosy, Journal of Chronic Disease 17:179-189, 1964.

Gussow, Z., Knight, E., and Miller, M.: A theory of leprosy stigma and professionalization of the patient role, unpublished paper, 1965, Department of Psychiatry, Louisiana State University Medical Center, New Orleans, Louisiana.

Gussow, Z., and Tracy, G.: Strategies in the management of stigma: concealing and revealing by leprosy patients in the U.S., unpublished paper, 1965, Department of Psychiatry, Louisiana State University Medical Center, New Orleans, Louisiana.

Hoffman, Joan: Nothing can be done: social dimensions of the treatment of stroke patients in a general hospital, Urban Life and Culture 3:50-70, 1974.

Kassenbaum, G., and Baumann, B.: Dimensions of the sick role in chronic illness, Journal of Health and Human Behavior 6:16-27, 1965.

Lenneberg, E., and Rowbotham, J.: The ileostomy patient, Springfield, Illinois, 1970, Charles C Thomas, Publisher.

Litman, Theodor: The family as a basic unit in health and medical care: a social-medical overview, Social Sciences and Medicine 8:495-519, 1974.

Louie, Theresa: The pragmatic context: a Chinese-American example of defining and managing illness, Ph.D. thesis, School of Nursing, University of California, San Francisco, 1975.

Quint, Jeanne: The impact of mastectomy, American Journal of Nursing 63:88-92, 1963.

Reif, Laura: A policy perspective and its implications, unpublished paper, Department of Social and Behavioral Science, School of Nursing, University of California, San Francisco.

Roth, Julius: Timetables: structuring the passage of time in hospital treatment and other careers, Indianapolis, 1963, The Bobbs-Merrill Co., Inc.

Schwartz, Charlotte: Strategies and tactics of mothers of mentally retarded children for dealing with the medical care system. In Bernstein, Norman, editor: Problems and care of the mentally retarded, Boston, 1970, Little, Brown & Co.

Strauss, Anselm, and Glaser, Barney: Anguish: case-history of a dying woman, San Francisco, 1970, Sociology Press.

Turk, J.: Impact of cystic fibrosis on family functioning, Pediatrics 34:67, 1964.

Wiener, Carolyn: Pain assessment, pain legitimation and the conflict of staff-patient perspectives, Nursing Outlook, 1975.

FIELD OBSERVATION AND INTERVIEWING

Filstead, William: Qualitative methodology: firsthand involvement with the social world, Chicago, 1970, Markham Publishing Co.

Glaser, Barney, and Strauss, Anselm: The discovery of grounded theory: strategies for qualitative research, Chicago, 1967, Aldine Publishing Co.

Gordon, Raymond: Interviewing: strategy, techniques and tactics, Homewood, Illinois, 1969, Dorsey Press.

Habenstein, Robert: Pathways to data: field methods for studying ongoing social organizations, Chicago, 1970, Aldine Publishing Co.

McCall, G., and Simmons, J.: Issues in participant observation: a text and reader, Reading, Massachusetts, 1969, Addison-Wesley Publishing Co., Inc.

Richardson, Stephen, Dorhrenwend, Barbara, and Klein, D.: Interviewing, its forms and functions, New York, 1965, Basic Books, Inc.

Schatzman, Leonard, and Strauss, Anselm: Field research: strategies for a natural sociology, Englewood Cliffs, New Jersey, 1973, Prentice-Hall, Inc.

Spindler, George, editor: Being an anthropologist, fieldwork in eleven cultures, New York, 1970, Holt, Rinehart and Winston, Inc.

Wax, Rosalie: Doing fieldwork: warnings and advice, Chicago, 1971, University of Chicago Press.

INDEX